FLORENCE LIN'S
Cooking with Fire Pots

Also by the author:

Florence Lin's Chinese Regional Cookbook
Florence Lin's Chinese Vegetarian Cookbook
Florence Lin's Chinese One-Dish Meals

FLORENCE LIN'S

Cooking with Fire Pots

by *Florence Lin*

with the assistance of Nai Gi

HAWTHORN BOOKS
A division of Elsevier-Dutton
New York

Library of Congress Catalog Card Number: 78-73331
ISBN: 0-8015-2671-X
1 2 3 4 5 6 7 8 9 10

Typographic Design by Judith Neuman

CONTENTS

FLORENCE LIN'S
Cooking with Fire Pots

All about Fire Pots

Traditional Chinese fire pots are festive, exotic, and hearty main dishes that consist of a great variety of ingredients and are usually served during cool or cold weather. The best-known examples are Chrysanthemum Fire Pot, Mongolian Fire Pot, and Ten Varieties Hot Pot. These meals are usually cooked and served at the table in a special centuries-old vessel known as a fire pot, a kind of Chinese fondue pot or chafing dish that allows for communal entertaining.

Fire pots may vary in size, shape, and material, but they all contain a large hollowed-out bowl, which holds broth and small (dipping-size) cuts of food, as well as a direct heating source. The simplest fire pots most closely resemble the chafing dish, and they are heated either by charcoal, alcohol, sterno, or electricity. More elaborate fire pots are fashioned from copper or brass and contain a small metal chimney that rises through the center of the bowl; these more sophisticated utensils resemble a "ring mold" or a bundt cake pan that rests atop a hollow base where the fuel (usually charcoal) is burned.

There are two different types of traditional fire pot dishes, but both types use either a good clear stock or a dense, gravylike sauce (usually spicy) as their base. The first type is composed of raw or partially cooked foods that finish cooking in the simmering broth or sauce. The techniques of eating and cooking the foods are similar to those employed with a meat fondue: small, very thinly sliced pieces of seafood, meat, and vegetables are presented at the table on separate platters. The diners, using chopsticks or fondue forks for spearing, select a piece of food, cook it briefly in the simmering broth, dip it into a salty sauce that both seasons and cools the food, then eat it immediately.

The second type of fire pot dish consists of a great variety of precooked ingredients, decoratively arranged in the broth. While the ingredients continue to simmer in the broth at a low heat, the diners help themselves, removing bits of food to individual rice bowls that may contain a couple of tablespoons of a dipping sauce. When all the food has been eaten, the cooking broth or sauce is served in the bowls at the end of the meal as the final course.

With a little ingenuity, the techniques of fire pot cooking can be applied to contemporary dishes for both everyday meals and special occasions. Contemporary fire pot dinners can either be prepared ahead or made on the spur of the moment, and if a fire pot vessel is unavailable, contemporary fire pot dishes can also be made and served in a casserole over a hot plate or in a variety of electrical appliances commonly found in most homes: deep fryers, slow cookers or crock pots, Dutch ovens, chafing dishes, fondue pots, skillets and frying pans, woks, and electric casseroles. An advantage to using one of these contemporary appliances is that it is easier to regulate the temperature, when, for example, you want to use moderate heat for precooked foods and higher heat for raw ingredients. If you decide to purchase a traditional, charcoal-burning fire pot, make certain that you use it in a well-ventilated room.

Whether you choose to prepare a traditional or contemporary fire pot dinner, you can save time and energy by following certain procedures. If your dish includes raw meat as an ingredient, it is important that the meat be cut into paper-thin slices. This job can be made easier if you partially freeze the meat, then slice it with a very sharp knife. Each place setting for a fire pot dinner should include a plate, a rice bowl, a soup spoon, a small dish for the dipping sauce, and either chopsticks or a long-handled fork. Bamboo chopsticks are easiest to handle when there are a large number of people present, but for informal occasions, bamboo skewers and fondue forks can be used for spearing the food, and there are thin-handled miniature utensils with wire baskets shaped like deep spoons that can also be used.

Many of the fire pot dishes in this book make hearty family meals that are particularly appropriate for the colder fall and winter months. They should be accompanied by rice, noodles, or buns. When fire pots are to be served at dinner parties, they should be preceded by a first course of appetizers, such as dim sum, cold plates, or light stir-fried dishes. If you serve cocktails before dinner, serve only platters of very light hors d'oeuvres, such as bowls of nuts. A dessert, either Western or Chinese, should complete the meal.

Fire pot dishes make any meal more festive and exciting because of the communal way of dining. Family meals become like indoor picnics, while company dinners are enhanced by the attractive and delicious foods presented at the table and by the drama of the dining style. Best of all, the host or hostess avoids cooking over a hot stove in a kitchen away from guests.

Since a good fire pot always depends on a good broth, stock, or sauce as its base, I have included information and recipes for making stocks at the beginning of this book. Recipes follow for the traditional fire pots, then contemporary main dish fire pots, light meals, and soups. The final section consists of recipes for dishes that may accompany fire pot dinners, such as sauces, dips, pastries, and buns.

Making a Good Stock

General Information

Stock is an important ingredient for all fire pots and soups. However, it is essential that every fire pot dish contain a stock with its own distinctive flavors. In order to give each stock its special flavor, stocks are made from a variety of ingredients—fowl, meat, meat with bones, as well as many kinds of vegetables. Sometimes a stock may be made from a combination of these ingredients. Some dishes require a rich and thick broth, while others need only a light and clear but flavorful stock.

When making a clear stock, the water must never come to more than a gentle boil, except during the beginning of the cooking and prior to the time when you skim off the foamy matter that rises to the surface. Once all the scum is removed, the heat is lowered and kept at a simmer. The pot is covered and the broth is simmered until done. Simmering means slow boiling of a liquid. One way of controlling the degree of slow boiling is by gauging the size of the bubbles that slowly rise from the bottom of the pot. There should be no bubbles larger than the size of a green pea. Another important factor in making a clear and smooth broth is the removal of all scum at the beginning of the cooking. If floating, foamy bubbles are not removed at the crucial early moments, they will be boiled into the broth. The broth will become cloudy with particles that cannot be removed while the broth is cooking. After the broth is cooked, it can be ladled or gently poured through a fine strainer or layers of cheesecloth.

To obtain a clear stock from meat and fowl, the meat and fowl can be blanched first by boiling in water for 5 minutes and then rinsed in cold water to remove all scum before cooking. Vegetables should not be blanched before making a stock.

Once a clear broth is made, it should be handled gently. To transfer the broth from one container to another, scoop it up with a large ladle or gently pour the stock into the container. Skim most of the fat off the top of the stock, but leave some to give the stock flavor. The stock can be refrigerated in a covered container for up to a week or frozen for up to 3 months.

CHI T'ANG
Chicken Stock

Read the general information (page 6) before making stock.

INGREDIENTS

1 5-pound fowl, cut into quarters
3 quarts cold water
1 scallion
1 teaspoon salt or to taste

PREPARATION

Place the chicken in a large pot with the cold water. Bring to a boil. Remove the foam and bubbles and keep the stock at a gentle boil until all the scum is removed. Lower the heat to a simmer, add the salt and scallion, cover the pot, and let it simmer for 3 hours. If the broth is kept at a simmer and is not allowed to reach a fast boil, the broth should be clear. The boiled chicken may be used for other dishes.

Yield: 10 cups chicken stock

Variations:

Other sizes and types of chicken or parts, such as a roasting chicken, back bones, or wings, may be used instead of fowl. For a rich stock, combine the chicken with pork, such as pork neck bones. Canned chicken broth and chicken bouillon cubes may be used instead of homemade chicken stock. Select the brands that contain only chicken flavor. Dilute each cup of canned chicken broth with ½ cup of water. Dissolve each bouillon cube as directed on the package.

JOU T'ANG
Pork, Beef, or Lamb Stock

Read the general information about making stock (page 6), as well as the cooking instructions for chicken stock (page 8), then use any of the following kinds of meat:

2 pounds pork neck bones or shoulder chops, 2 pounds beef neck or shank bones or stewing beef with bones, or 2 pounds stewing lamb with bones (use only American spring lamb)

INGREDIENTS

To any one of the above kinds of meat add the following ingredients:
3   quarts cold water
1/4 cup dry sherry
1   scallion
1   teaspoon salt

PREPARATION

Rinse the meat and bones in cold water before cooking. Cook the meat stock in the same manner as the chicken stock, only instead of cooking the stock for 3 hours, cook the meat and bones for 5 hours. Discard the bones and use the boiled meat for other dishes.

Yield: 8 cups meat stock

Note:

For a rich stock, combine pork with chicken.

SU TS'AI T'ANG
Vegetable Stock or Soup

This simple vegetable soup has a clear and refreshing flavor. Adding the oil at the end makes this soup tastier. We call it *"pu yu."*

INGREDIENTS

1   pound cabbage, cut into 1-inch pieces
2   medium carrots, sliced
1   medium potato, peeled and cut into small cubes
1½ teaspoons salt or to taste
2   tablespoons peanut or corn oil

PREPARATION

In a large pot, combine the cabbage, carrots, potato, salt, and 6 cups water, and bring to a boil. Cook the vegetables at a low heat for 1½ hours. If you wish to make a stock, allow the vegetables and broth to cool, then drain off the liquid and reserve it for stock. It can be used as a vegetarian soup base. Save the solid ingredients for other uses. If you wish to make a vegetable soup, add the oil to the vegetables and liquid and serve hot.

Yield: 6 servings as soup

Variations:

For extra flavor, add ½ pound sliced fresh mushrooms to the soup. Other greens such as celery, green beans, peppers, peas, or green-leaf vegetables may be added to or used in place of the cabbage and carrots. Sauté 2

medium-size tomatoes, cut into sections, in 3 tablespoons oil, and add to the soup just before serving. Cook the soup for 3 minutes. The tomatoes will color the oil red. Omit the previously listed 2 tablespoons oil. For a richer and stronger-flavored soup, sauté 1 sliced medium-size onion with oil. Separately sauté all the vegetables, including the tomato, with more oil. Add boiling water, bring to a boil, cover, and cook over low heat for 2 hours.

CHIANG YU T'ANG
Soy Sauce Broth

This economical and instant broth can be used as a soup for a meal or as a basic broth in the fire pot, to which will be added other ingredients.

INGREDIENTS

2¹/₂ tablespoons light soy sauce
1¹/₂ tablespoons sesame oil
¹/₄ teaspoon monosodium glutamate
2 teaspoons minced scallion
¹/₈ teaspoon white pepper
4 cups boiling water

PREPARATION

This soup can be served in a large serving bowl, in which case place all the ingredients in the bowl and pour the boiling water over the ingredients. This soup can also be served in a fire pot, or as a cook-and-serve casserole; bring the water to a boil in the fire pot or casserole and then add all the seasoning ingredients.

Yield: 4 servings

Note:

Dried laver (dried purple seaweed) may be added to the soup. The laver comes in thin sheets, 8 × 8 inches. Do not cook it. Tear one sheet into small pieces and add to the bowl along with the other seasonings before adding the boiling water.

The Traditional Fire Pots

CHÜ HUA KUO
(TA PIEN LU)
Chrysanthemum Fire Pot

Cantonese fire pots, like all fire pots, are served in cool weather. Chrysanthemum pot and *ta pien lu* are two fire pots that originated in Canton. They both have similar ingredients, which include meat, poultry, organ meats, vegetables, and a lot of seafood. The raw ingredients are brought to the table and cooked while dining. The chrysanthemum fire pot, which is named after the seasonal flower, is better known throughout the different regions of China, and it is the more sophisticated of the two fire pots. It is more intricately decorated, and is arranged with garnishes, such as coriander. In China, the flower petals of the white chrysanthemum are used to season the soup, and they provide a refreshing flavor. But in the United States it is unsafe to eat these flower petals, nor should they be used to flavor foods, because it is likely that they have been sprayed with insecticide. Although a chrysanthemum fire pot makes a hearty one-dish meal for families, for company dinners either plates of cold hors d'oeuvres or light stir-fried appetizers should precede the serving of the fire pot as the main course.

INGREDIENTS

Fire Pot:

1   large whole chicken breast, skinned and boned, semifrozen then cut into thin 2 × 2-inch slices
1   pound sirloin or flank steak, semifrozen then cut into very thin 2 × 2-inch slices
1   pound fresh shrimp, shelled, deveined, and split laterally into halves
1/2 pound fillet of gray sole, scrod, or yellow pike, cut into 1 × 2 × 1/2-inch slices
1   dozen shucked clams, on the half shell with juice
1/4 pound calf's or chicken liver, sliced into 1 × 2 × 1/4-inch pieces

1 teaspoon salt
1/4 teaspoon white pepper
2 teaspoons dry sherry
2 teaspoons peanut or corn oil
1/2 cup coriander leaves and tender stems
2 ounces cellophane noodles, softened in boiling water for 20 minutes
1/2 pound fresh tender spinach or lettuce, rinsed well and drained
1 large piece fresh tender bean curd, cut into 2 × 1 × 1/2-inch slices
8 cups chicken stock, page 8
1 large chrysanthemum, for decoration

Sauce:

2 eggs
1/2 teaspoon sugar
3 tablespoons light soy sauce
2 tablespoons dry sherry
1 tablespoon oyster sauce
1 tablespoon sesame oil
1 tablespoon minced scallion

PREPARATION On two platters or six plates, arrange (and alternate) the cut chicken, beef, shrimp, fish, and clams in one overlapping layer. Season with the salt, pepper, sherry, and oil. Cover the plates with plastic wrap and refrigerate until serving time. Drain the cellophane noodles and put them along with the spinach and bean curd into two serving bowls. Store the coriander in a plastic bag until serving time, when it will be used to garnish the meat and fish.

To make the sauce, beat the eggs thoroughly, then add the remaining sauce ingredients and mix well. Pour a couple tablespoons of the sauce into individual rice bowls; the sauce will be used as a dip either before or after cooking the meat. If the meat is dipped into the sauce before cooking, the egg coating and seasonings will give the meat a smooth and tender consistency. If the meat is dipped into the sauce after it is cooked, the sauce seasons and cools the meat.

AT THE TABLE   Pour the chicken stock into either a traditional fire pot or an electric casserole or Dutch oven and place the appliance on the dining table. Bring the stock to a boil. The stock must remain at a slow, continuous boil while it cooks the raw ingredients.

Place 6 individual rice bowls containing the sauce on the table. Put the meat, fish, and vegetables on the table and allow each person to serve himself, holding chopsticks in one hand and the sauce bowl in the other.

Using chopsticks or a fork to skewer a piece of the meat, fish, shrimp, clam, or chicken, each person may dip the ingredient into either the sauce or the boiling stock and cook it until it appears done or the ingredients may be removed from the pot and then dipped into the sauce. Eat each piece as soon as it is cooked. In general, after the meat and seafood are consumed, the vegetables and the remaining ingredients are then added to the broth and cooked all together. After they are cooked, the solid ingredients are removed with chopsticks and placed in the rice bowls. The broth is then ladled into the same sauce bowls with the rice. However, there are no set rules; the fire pot ingredients may be eaten in any order desired.

Yield: 6 servings

Note:

The traditional chrysanthemum fire pot sometimes is served as a soup at the end of a formal banquet. It usually contains comparatively small amounts of raw ingredients, and they are put into the fire pot all at once. As soon as the ingredients are cooked, the hot soup is served and eaten. Chrysanthemum fire pot provides a special finishing touch to any formal banquet.

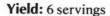

SHUAN YANG JOU
Mongolian Fire Pot

Mongolian fire pot consists of lamb slices that are cooked in a hearty lamb stock. Later, vegetables and bean curd are added to the stock. The blend of different flavors from the various ingredients makes this fire pot dish an exquisite eating experience, especially during cold winter months.

INGREDIENTS

Fire Pot:

3 to 4 pounds leg of American spring lamb
4 ounces cellophane noodles, soaked in boiling water for 20 minutes
1/2 pound fresh tender spinach, rinsed well
1/2 pound heart of celery cabbage, cut into 2 × 1-inch pieces
1 large piece fresh bean curd, cut into 2 × 1-inch pieces
8 cups lamb stock, page 9

Sauce:

6 tablespoons peanut butter, diluted with 6 tablespoons warm water
1 tablespoon red or white fermented bean curd or 1/2 teaspoon salt
1/4 cup light soy sauce
2 tablespoons sesame oil
2 tablespoons dry sherry
2 tablespoons cider vinegar
1 tablespoon sugar
1/2 to 1 teaspoon ground red chili pepper combined with 2 teaspoons corn oil
    or 1/2 to 1 teaspoon prepared red chili oil
1/4 cup cold water
1 scallion, finely chopped

1 teaspoon finely chopped garlic
1/4 cup chopped coriander leaves and tender stems
12 *Chih ma shao ping* (sesame seed pastries), page 113

PREPARATION

Remove the bones and tendons from the leg of lamb, reserving them for the stock (page 9). Dress the red meat with string as for a roast and keep it in the freezer until it is slightly frozen. Remove the string and use an electric slicer or a sharp Chinese cleaver, or ask your butcher to trim, freeze, and slice the lamb for you. Slice the meat into paper-thin 2 × 4-inch pieces. Before it thaws, arrange and overlap the meat slices on 6 small plates. This can be done ahead of time. Cover with plastic wrap, stack the plates, and refrigerate them until serving time.

Drain off the excess water from the softened cellophane noodles and put them on two serving platters along with the spinach, celery cabbage, and bean curd.

To make the sauce, mix the peanut butter with warm water in a bowl until it becomes a thin paste. Then add the remaining sauce ingredients. If you wish to make the sauce ahead of time, leave out the scallion, garlic, and coriander and add these ingredients just before serving time. Pour the sauce into individual rice bowls (about 2 tablespoons of sauce per bowl), replenishing when necessary.

AT THE TABLE

If you do not have a traditional fire pot, use either an electric casserole, a Dutch oven, or a deep fryer. Place the appliance on the dining table, add the lamb stock, and bring it to a boil. Place the plates of lamb slices, vegetables, and sesame seed pastries around the fire pot. The broth must be kept at a continuous simmer or gentle boil. The intensity of the heat will vary depending upon the number of pieces of lamb that are being cooked. Each person should cook his own lamb slices, holding the meat with chopsticks or a long fork and dipping the slices into the boiling broth. When a slice is cooked, the person removes it from the stock and dips it into the prepared sauce. The sauce seasons the lamb and at the same time cools it. Serve the sesame seed pastries along with the lamb.

After all the lamb is consumed, the vegetables should be cooked in the lamb broth. Add the prepared vegetables, bean curd, and cellophane noodles, cover and cook briefly. To serve, use chopsticks to serve the noodles and vegetables in the individual rice bowls. Then ladle out the soup into each bowl. You may season the vegetables with the remaining sauce.

Yield: 6 servings as a main course

Variations:

Top sirloin beef may be used instead of lamb. Pita or a crusty French or Italian bread may be used instead of sesame seed pastries.

SHIH CHING NUAN KUO
Ten Varieties Hot Pot

This elaborate dish, which originated in the eastern region of China, is traditionally served in winter. It consists of assorted precooked meat, seafood, eggs, wheat gluten, vegetables, and soybean products. Not every ingredient listed needs to be included, but the hot pot will taste better if it includes all of the basic ingredients. The cook's choice of selected additional ingredients should be determined by the availability of ingredients for creating a variety of different tastes, the number of servings, and the type of occasion.

INGREDIENTS

Basic hot pot:

2 ounces cellophane noodles, softened in boiling water for 20 minutes
6 large dried mushrooms, soaked in warm water; after removing and discarding stems, cut into halves
1 pound heart of celery cabbage, cut lengthwise into 3 × 1½-inch pieces, parboiled
½ cup sliced fresh or canned bamboo shoots, cut into 1 × 2 × ⅛-inch pieces
½ cup sliced cooked Smithfield ham, cut into 1 × 2 × ⅛-inch pieces
6 to 8 cups chicken stock, page 8
1½ teaspoons salt or to taste

Selected additions:

12 cooked fish balls, page 78
12 cooked meat balls, page 65
12 cooked shrimp balls, page 75
1 cup cooked pork, page 93, or chicken, page 94
1 cooked pork egg roll, page 62, cut diagonally into 12 slices

1 dozen small clams, brushed clean and soaked in salt water (1 teaspoon salt per cup fresh water) for 3 to 4 hours
12 fried wheat gluten balls, page 105
2 small pieces firm bean curd, frozen and then thawed and cut into 1-inch pieces

AT THE TABLE
A traditional fire pot, chafing dish, crock pot, electric frying pan, skillet, deep fryer, or Dutch oven can be used for this hot pot.

Drain the cellophane noodles well. Place the cabbage in the fire pot and then arrange a layer of cellophane noodles on top of the cabbage. Add the bamboo shoots, ham slices, mushroom halves, and the cooked meats and seafoods, arranging all the ingredients in a decorative pattern over the cellophane noodles. Then add your choice of ingredients from the list of selected additions. Pour the chicken stock over all. Cover, bring to a boil, and simmer for 10 minutes before serving. If the pot is not large enough for all the ingredients, replenish with ingredients and stock and continue to cook while you eat. If a crock pot or slow cooker is used, preheat the stock before adding it to the pot. Gently pour in the chicken stock, adding just enough to fill up to the food level. Cover the crock pot and bring the stock to a boil. If clams are used, cook them until they open, about 10 minutes. Serve piping hot. Keep the pot simmering hot until everyone has finished eating. (Hence the name of this dish.) Individual bowls of rice and small dishes of soy sauce (to be used as a dip) should accompany ten varieties hot pot.

Yield: 6 servings as a main dish

MAO TU HUO KUO
Peppery Tripe Fire Pot

This Szechuan fire pot is served in small, informal roadside restaurants throughout western China. *Mao tu* consists of partially cooked honeycomb cow's tripe dipped into a concentrated spicy sauce that is traditionally cooked in a clay pot over a charcoal-burning mud stove. The pot stands high on the table so that people stand and eat rather than sit on benches. If people get tired from standing, they put their foot on the bench and lean forward against the knee and eat in that position. It is a very casual way of eating. This dish can also be cooked in a traditional fire pot.

INGREDIENTS

Fire Pot:

2   pounds partially cooked tripe
1/2 pound calf's liver
1   pound top sirloin or flank steak, partially frozen for easier slicing
1/2 pound calf's brain
4   1-inch pieces of beef bone marrow
1/2 pound bok choy or celery cabbage, cut into 1 × 2-inch pieces and parboiled
1/2 pound cooked noodles, any kind
2   scallions, cut into 2-inch pieces

Sauce:

3   cups concentrated beef stock or canned undiluted beef broth
1   teaspoon Szechuan peppercorns
4   thin slices fresh gingerroot
1   teaspoon crushed red chili pepper

1 teaspoon salt-fermented black beans, rinsed in water and mashed
3 tablespoons brown bean sauce
1/2 teaspoon salt
1 teaspoon rock or cane sugar
2 tablespoons dry sherry

PREPARATION

Trim the fat off the tripe and cut it into 1 × 2-inch strips. Blanch the tripe in a pot of boiling water for 2 minutes. Drain and squeeze several times to rinse well. In a heavy pot, cook the tripe with 4 cups of water over low heat for about 2 hours, or until it is tender but still crisp (check its texture after 1 hour of cooking). Cool, drain, discard the water, and squeeze the tripe dry. Place the tripe pieces on 2 plates, allowing space for the liver and beef. Cut the calf's liver into 1 × 2-inch slices and blanch in boiling water for 2 minutes. Drain well and set aside on the same plates with the tripe. Cut the partially frozen beef into 2 × 2-inch paper-thin slices and overlap the slices on the plates. Remove the outermost blood vessels and membrane from the calf's brain with a bamboo skewer. Using the point of the skewer, pick up the membrane and pull it off with your fingers or roll it off with the skewer. In this way, you can remove all of the vessels and membranes. Poach the brain in boiling water for 3 minutes. Gently transfer it into a pot of cold water to cool. Then cut the brain into 1-inch pieces, discarding any loose pieces. Set aside with the bone marrow and scallions on another plate.

Parboil the bok choy or cabbage and noodles and place them in a bowl. Cover with plastic wrap and store in the refrigerator. All of the ingredients can be prepared in advance.

AT THE TABLE Allow 20 minutes before serving time. Start the fire pot by adding the sauce ingredients and let them boil for 5 minutes. Add the scallions, calf's brain, and bone marrow, and cook for 15 minutes. The marrow will become a part of the sauce, while the brain becomes soft and smooth and should be eaten with the meat. At serving time, place the plates of meat and the bowl with vegetables and noodles near the fire pot. With a pair of bamboo chopsticks or a fork, take a piece of beef, tripe, or liver, dip it into the spicy sauce in the fire pot, and cook it for a few seconds. Using a rice bowl to catch the drippings, hold the meat above the bowl until it cools a bit. When all the meat slices are consumed, add the vegetables and noodles to the sauce. Just heat through, then remove them with chopsticks into individual rice bowls. Ladle the sauce into the bowls and eat the sauce soup.

Yield: 4 servings as a main course

Contemporary Fire Pots as Main Courses

YI P'IN KUO
Treasure Casserole

This is an elaborate casserole that has casually and disrespectfully been referred to by some as "Buddha Jumped over the Fence." This name comes from a story about how this dish's irresistible aroma caused even Buddha to break his vows of vegetarianism and to "jump over the fence" to taste the dish.

Treasure casserole is usually prepared during the New Year holidays when there are large gatherings of families and friends eating together. Different kinds of meat, poultry, and seafood, both fresh and dried, are used. Some ingredients require days of soaking or steaming before they are ready for the final cooking. When it is time to cook, the ingredients are placed in a large (traditionally earthenware) pot and slowly steamed or simmered into a sumptuous soup. This dish can also be made in a fire pot, an electric casserole, or most other electrical appliances.

Ingredients rich in gelatin are combined with medicinal herbs and other ingredients that simply give good flavor. Some people overdo the medicinal ingredients because they believe that you should eat this soup as a tonic to start off the winter right. But one should use discretion and remember that this casserole is a very good soup, and it must not end up tasting like a bowl of Chinese herbal medicine.

To make this casserole into a more sophisticated, special dish, exotic ingredients can be cooked in an antique earthenware vessel. The treasure casserole requires four basic ingredients: an unseasoned meat, which is usually pork; a seasoned pork, such as Smithfield-type ham; poultry, which may be duck, chicken, or squab; and a vegetable, such as celery cabbage, winter mushrooms, or fresh bamboo shoots. When combined, the four basic ingredients themselves make a delicious soup; and when the soup is served with rice, it becomes a hot, hearty winter meal.

Many more ingredients may be added, and I have categorized them according to whether they supply texture, flavor, or medicinal effects. The foods that impart texture but no flavor of their own take up flavor from the broth. Examples include shark's fin, sea cucumber, fish maw, deer tendon, and chu sheng (Szechuan bamboo-shoot flowers). The latter actually are not bamboo-shoot flowers at all but a kind of mushroom that is grown in bamboo forests. Dried squid, scallops, abalone, and dried Chinese mushrooms provide both taste and texture. Ginseng from Korea, *kou chi* seeds (*Lysium chinense*, a shrub grown in certain areas of the United States), meat, and the skin found at the edge of the sea turtle's shell are a few ingredients that provide tonic effects.

Only a few of the ingredients have been mentioned, and there are many more. When the elaborate version of this dish is cooked, the basic ingredients are sometimes removed after the cooking is completed; only the broth is served with the exotic ingredients.

BASIC TREASURE CASSEROLE INGREDIENTS

1 pound Smithfield ham, uncooked
1 fresh pork shoulder or fresh ham, about 3 pounds
1 chicken, duck, or 2 squabs, about 4 pounds
1 pound celery cabbage heart, cut into 2-inch sections
2 scallions
2 tablespoons dry sherry
2 teaspoons salt or to taste

PREPARATION

Soak the Smithfield ham in cold water for 2 hours. Wash and scrape off the pepper from the skin side of the ham. Trim off the discolored part from the flesh side of the ham and remove any bone marrow. Rinse well in water to remove every speck of pepper.

Place the pork shoulder, the ham, and scallions in a large pot, and add water to cover. Bring the water to a boil and skim off the scum. Lower the heat to a slow simmer and cook for 1 hour. Remove the ham and allow it to cool. Cook the pork for 1 more hour.

Blanch the poultry in boiling water for 5 minutes. When the pork has cooked for 2 hours, transfer it with its liquid to either a large electric or nonelectric casserole. Add the blanched chicken and enough boiling water to cover the chicken and pork, but allow room for the vegetables to be added later. Bring the contents to a boil and skim off any foam that appears. Add the sherry. Cover and put into a preheated 250° oven (if an electric casserole is used, turn heat to 250°) and cook 1 hour. Add the celery cabbage sections, cut side up in the center of the casserole, and add the salt. Cover and cook for 1 more hour. All the ingredients in the casserole should be very tender. If not, cook a little longer. This soup takes about 4 hours to cook. Just before serving, remove the scallions and skim the fat. Cut the cooled ham into thin slices, and arrange the slices in a decorative pattern around the celery cabbage. Serve piping hot.

ELABORATE TREASURE CASSEROLE

Using the basic treasure casserole recipe ingredients minus the vegetables, put them in a large pot. Add water to cover and bring to a boil, skimming off the scum. Lower the heat to a simmer, cover, and cook for 4 hours. If the casserole is cooked properly and not allowed to come to a fast boil, the broth should remain clear. The meat and poultry should be very tender and almost falling apart. Gently drain off the broth. The broth is to be used for the stock of the elaborate treasure casserole. The leftover cooked ingredients may be saved for other dishes as salads.

Select at least two or three ingredients from the following three groups, or choose an unlimited amount of ingredients from the following list and prepare each well in advance before combining and cooking them together. Different ingredients require different preparation and cooking times, so plan to prepare ingredients that require the longest times first, then schedule the addition of the other ingredients accordingly. It is best to read through the entire recipe before proceeding.

Texture	Flavor	Tonic
shark's fin	the basic stock	the basic stock
sea cucumber	squid	shark's fin
fish maw	scallops	sea cucumber
deer tendon	abalone	fish maw
squid	sea turtle	deer tendon
scallops	winter mushrooms	ginseng
abalone	fresh bamboo shoots	*kou chi* seeds
winter mushrooms		sea turtle
fresh bamboo shoots		
chu sheng (Szechuan bamboo-shoot flowers)		

Shark's fin:

One whole dried shark's fin must be soaked in cold water for about 3 days. Rinse and remove any skin, bone, or flesh attached to the base of the fin. Put the cleaned fin in a crock pot, cover with water, and add a 1-inch slice of gingerroot. Cover the pot and cook for 8 hours. Drain off the water, discarding the gingerroot. Rinse the shark's fin under cold running water, being careful not to disturb the shape of the fin. Set the fin in a bowl. Add 1 tablespoon dry sherry, 1/8 teaspoon white pepper, and enough chicken broth to cover. Steam the dish over medium heat for about 1 hour. Drain off and discard the liquid and reserve the fin. It is now ready to be added to the casserole and be cooked for another hour.

Fish maw:

Soak 2 ounces fish maw (fish's air bladder, the prepared and already puffed kind) in cold water for 30 minutes, using a plate to weigh down the soaking fish maw. Bring the fish maw and water to a boil. Add a 1-inch slice of gingerroot, 1 tablespoon dry sherry, and $1/8$ teaspoon white pepper. Remove from the heat and, using a large spoon, stir around several times. Allow to cool, and then squeeze out all the water with your hand and cut the fish maw into $1/2 \times 11/2$-inch strips. It is now ready to be added to the casserole and cooked for another 30 minutes.

Sea cucumber (sea slug or *bêche-de-mer*):

If a large sea cucumber is used, scorch its surface over an open fire until it is black. Scrape off the black part and rinse well. Put the sea cucumber in a large pot with water to cover. Cover and bring to a boil. Remove from the heat and soak until it is completely cool. Use a knife to cut open the sea cucumber lengthwise. Remove the innards and wash and clean the body inside and out. Put it back into the pot with clean water, bring it to a boil, and let it soak again. This may be repeated once more or until the sea cucumber is quite soft. Rinse the softened sea cucumber under cold running water for a few hours, so that the sticky residue is rinsed off. Or let it soak in cold water for 1 day and change the water several times. The sea cucumber may be cut into 1×2-inch pieces and is now ready to be added to the casserole. It will need to cook for another 30 minutes.

Dried abalone:

Soak 4 dried abalone with cold water at least 4 to 5 hours or overnight. Drain and brush the outside of the abalone. Place in a saucepan and cover with cold water. Bring to a boil, add 1 scallion and a 1-inch slice of gingerroot. Use a plate to weigh down the abalone. Cover and cook over very low heat for up to 20 hours. If the abalone are large, slice them; if they are small, score them. Put them back into the original liquid. The abalone are now ready to be added to the casserole along with the liquid. Just cook enough to heat through; too high a heat or long cooking will make them tough again.

Dried squid:

Using 1 or 2 medium-size squids, soak in cold water overnight. Drain and rinse under cold running water, pull and discard the brownish-black outer skin, as well as the internal cartilage. Remove the head. Use only the body, the fins, and the firm tentacles attached to the head of the squid. Soak the cleaned squid for about 2 days in 4 cups of cold water into which 2 tablespoons baking soda has been added and dissolved. Cover the container and refrigerate during the soaking. Drain, and repeat procedure again with fresh water and soda. Soak for 2 more days or until your finger nail can dig into the flesh easily. Score the body meat in a crisscross pattern on the internal side, then cut into 1 × 2-inch pieces. Soak them in cold water for 1 day, change the water several times, or let water run over the squid for 2 hours to get rid of the soda taste. (The softened squid can be kept in a container with cold water in the refrigerator for 2 to 3 days.) It is now ready to be put into the casserole and cooked for 5 minutes.

Deer tendon:

Cook 6 to 8 tendons, covered with 2 inches of water, in a slow cooker. Add 1 scallion, a 1-inch slice of gingerroot, and 2 tablespoons dry sherry. Cook for 2 days. Drain and discard all the ingredients but the tendons. Add enough chicken broth to cover the tendons and continue cooking for 1 more day. Drain off the chicken broth, add the tendons to the casserole, and cook for 2 more hours.

Dried scallops:

Use 4 ounces large dried scallops and soak in 1 cup warm water for 2 hours. Add 2 tablespoons dry sherry to the scallops and steam for 30 minutes or until very tender. They are now ready to be added to the casserole and need to cook for only 5 minutes.

Ginseng:

Use 2 ounces of sliced ginseng without any additional preparation. Just put into the casserole and let it cook for 1 hour. Or steam the ginseng with 1 cup of water for 4 hours, add the liquid to the casserole, and discard the ginseng slices.

Dried *kou chi* seeds (*Lysium chinense*):

Add 2 tablespoons dried seeds to the casserole and cook for 2 hours.

Chu sheng (Szechuan bamboo-shoot flowers):

Soak 4 dried bamboo-shoot flowers in cold water for 4 hours. Rinse in warm water several times, then squeeze dry. Cut each into 2-inch pieces. They are now ready to be added to the casserole and need to cook for 1 hour.

Sea turtle:

Cut up the sea turtle into 8 pieces, blanch in boiling water, drain, and discard the water. Put the turtle pieces in a large heatproof bowl. Add water to cover and 2 1-inch slices of gingerroot, 2 scallions, and 2 cups rice wine. Cover and steam the bowl within a large pot over medium-low heat for 4 hours. Drain the broth through a fine strainer discarding the solids. The broth is ready to be added to the casserole and needs to cook for 30 minutes. The skin of the edge of the turtle's shell is considered by many to be a fine delicacy; after 2 hours of steaming, remove the skin. It can be added to the casserole and cooked for another 30 minutes.

Dried winter mushrooms:

Soak 10 winter mushrooms in warm water for 1 hour or until they are very soft. Remove and discard the stems. Drain and save the soaking water, discarding the sediment. The mushrooms and soaking water can be added to the casserole and cooked for 2 hours.

Fresh winter bamboo shoots:

Using 2 or 3 winter bamboo shoots, peel the brown, fuzzy exterior shells and cut off any loose parts. Cut the flesh of the peeled bamboo shoots into halves, then cut lengthwise into thin slices. These can be directly added to the casserole and cooked for 30 minutes.

SHA KUO YU TOU
Earthenware Pot Fish Head Stew

The traditional Chinese way of eating a fish head is to serve it in an earthenware pot. The pot is carried directly from the stove to the table while it is still bubbling, since this dish tastes best when it is eaten piping hot. The fire pot and electric casserole are perfect substitute appliances to use when serving this dish because they will continue to keep the ingredients warm if you decide to eat directly from them.

It is important that the fish head used in this dish be very fresh, or if it's frozen, the fish head must be very fresh at the time of freezing. If a very large fish head is used, use half of it and freeze the other half for another meal.

INGREDIENTS

1	2-pound fish head from striped bass, tile or cod fish, or any white fish with a collar and some flesh on the back part of the head, as long as it's not an oily fish
1/2	teaspoon salt
	Flour for dredging
4	tablespoons peanut or corn oil
2	scallions, cut into 2-inch sections
2	1/2-inch slices gingerroot, crushed
2	cloves garlic, crushed
1/4	teaspoon Szechuan peppercorns
1	tablespoon brown bean sauce
3	tablespoons dark soy sauce

2   tablespoons dry sherry
1   tablespoon cider vinegar
2   teaspoons sugar
2   cups chicken stock, page 8, or canned chicken broth
2   ounces cellophane noodles, soaked in boiling water for 20 minutes
1/4 tcaspoon white pepper

PREPARATION

Ask the fish cleaner to remove the gills and scales, if any, from the fish head. Rinse and dry it thoroughly. Sprinkle the salt inside of the head and over the flesh. Dredge it in flour and shake off the excess. Heat a wok until very hot. Add one tablespoon oil to coat the wok, then turn off the heat and let it cool. When the wok is complctely cooled, turn the heat on again and add the remaining 3 tablespoons oil. The above procedure of turning on and off the heat is to treat the wok, so that when the fish head is fried it will not stick. Fry the fish head over medium heat for 10–15 minutes on each side or until lightly brown. Push the fish head to the side, and add the gingerroot, garlic, scallions, and peppercorns, and let them brown a bit. Transfer the entire contents of the wok to a fire pot or a cook-and-serve casserole. Add the remaining ingredients except the cellophane noodles and white pepper. Up to this point, this dish can be prepared ahead of time. Bring it to a boil and cook over low heat for 30 minutes.

AT THE TABLE

Drain the cellophane noodles and add to the fire pot or casserole. Bring the dish to the table, cover, and cook for 10 minutes. The flesh from the fish

head will fall away from the head with chopsticks. Season with white pepper and serve very hot with plain rice or steamed buns in individual rice bowls or soup plates.

Yield: 4 servings as a main course

Variations:

Instead of cellophane noodles, 2 pieces of bean curd may be used. Instead of one fish head, an entire fish including the head may be used.

CHI PAO YEN WO T'ANG
Boneless Chicken Soup with Bird's Nest Stuffing

Bird's nests are a Chinese delicacy often used in fancier soups. They are made from seaweed that has been chewed by swiflets. These nests are built prior to egg-laying on rocky cliffs and in caves along the shores of the Pacific Ocean throughout the South Pacific coasts and inlands. They reach the market in various states, some are whole and in the shape of a large flower petal, while others are loose. Some are even cleaned, precooked, and packaged, and are ready to be used in soups without further preparation. Depending on the quality of these nests, they can be very expensive. Others are more reasonable in cost. The texture also varies; some are soft and others are crunchy. The whole ones that have a softer texture are considered to be of better quality and, of course, they are more expensive.

INGREDIENTS

3 ounces bird's nests
1 3 to 4-pound chicken, preferably fresh-killed
4 cups chicken stock, page 8
2 teaspoons salt
1 scallion
1 1-inch slice gingerroot
1/4 teaspoon white pepper

PREPARATION   Soak the bird's nests in warm water for at least 4 hours. For easier cleaning use a white bowl and remove the minute debris and down that will float in the water. Hold nests in a fine sieve and rinse very well. Place in a saucepan with 2 cups cold water and bring to a boil and cook for 2 minutes. Drain off the water and rinse the softened bird's nests again, then squeeze dry gently. You will have about 2 cups.

To bone the chicken:

Wash and dry the chicken. Fold back the neck skin as far as it will go. Using a sharp knife or kitchen shears, make tiny cuts or snips against the bones under the flesh, starting with the wish bone and slowly working down. Do not bone the wings, but cut them off at the shoulder joint; wiggle the wings to find the joints and sever them at the shoulder. Use extra care not to pierce the skin while freeing the back. As you work, always cut against the bones. Detach the legs, remove the thigh bones and half of the drumstick bones, leaving the flesh intact with the skin. Work in the same manner up to the tail bone. Do not remove the tail; leave it attached to the skin but sever it at the base of the spine. At this point the entire chicken is boned, leaving the skin, tail, drumsticks, and wings intact with the flesh. Sprinkle with 1 teaspoon salt on the flesh, then turn the boned chicken skin-side out.

To stuff the chicken:

Close the neck opening with a 4-inch skewer. Spoon the cleaned bird's nests through the tail opening. When stuffed, close this opening with another skewer.

Use a bowl large enough to hold both the chicken and the 4 cups of stock; it should only be three quarters full. Add the remaining 1 teaspoon salt, scallion, and gingerroot.

To steam the chicken soup:

Place the bowl with the chicken soup in a large pot with a rack. The pot must be large enough so that when the soup is cooked, it can be removed easily while it is still very hot.

Add boiling water to the pot along the sides of the bowl. Bring it up to $1^{1}/_{2}$ inches below the outer rim of the bowl. Cover the pot and bring the water to a boil over high heat, turn heat down to low and let steam for 2 hours. Replenish with boiling water when necessary. The chicken should be very tender and the broth should be crystal clear. Remove the scallion and gingerroot, and skim off the fat. Sprinkle with white pepper.

AT THE TABLE   The soup can be brought to the table in a fire pot or casserole. Serve piping hot in individual bowls.

Yield: 8 servings as soup

KEN SZE T'ANG
Chicken, Ham, and Shrimp
with Pressed Bean Curd

INGREDIENTS

4 3 × 3 × ¹/₂-pieces *pai tou fu kan* (plain pressed bean curd)
4 cups boiling water
¹/₂ teaspoon baking soda
1 chicken breast
4 dried mushrooms, soaked in hot water for 30 minutes
¹/₂ cup finely shredded bamboo shoots
¹/₄ cup finely shredded cooked Smithfield ham
¹/₂ pound fresh shrimp, shelled, deveined, and diced
1¹/₂ teaspoons salt
¹/₂ teaspoon cornstarch
1 tablespoon dry sherry
2 tablespoons peanut or corn oil
1 small scallion, finely shredded
6 cups pork stock, page 9, or chicken stock, page 8, with some fat remaining

PREPARATION

Cut the pressed bean curd pieces into paper-thin slices, then cut the slices into very fine strips. Pour the 4 cups boiling water into a large bowl and add the baking soda; mix well. Add the cut-up bean curd strips, and let them soak for 5 minutes. Drain and soak them in warm water. Meanwhile, add the chicken breast and 2 cups of water to a saucepan. Cover, bring to a boil, and boil for 10 minutes. With the cover still on, turn off the heat, and let the chicken cool in the water. During the slow cooling of the hot water, the chicken becomes completely cooked. Remove the bones of the chicken and cut the chicken breast meat into fine strips with the grain. Set aside on a plate. Put the bones and skin back into the water and cook some more. Drain the broth, remove the solid matter, and reserve the broth for use in the future. Drain the mushrooms, remove and discard the stems, then cut them into very fine strips, and set aside on a plate along with the cut-up bamboo shoots and ham.

Combine the diced shrimp with ½ teaspoon salt and the cornstarch. Mix well and refrigerate for 30 minutes. Stir-fry the shrimp in 2 tablespoons oil for 30 seconds, add the scallion and mix well. Dish out and set aside.

AT THE TABLE Drain off the water from the bean curd strips and put into a fire pot or a cook-and-serve casserole along with the chicken, ham, bamboo shoots, and mushrooms. Add the remaining teaspoon salt, sherry, and the stock. Bring the liquid to a boil, lower the heat, and simmer for ½ hour. Add the shrimp just before serving.

Yield: 4 servings as a meal, 8 servings as a soup

Variation:

To make this a vegetarian soup, use snow pea pods, fresh mushrooms, and carrots cut in the same manner as the chicken, ham, and shrimp. Use vegetable stock (page 10) instead of meat or chicken stock.

HUO T'UI CH'UAN CHI T'ANG
Chicken and Ham Soup

The whole chicken cooked until tender with Smithfield ham gives this soup its special flavor. If the chicken is slowly cooked at just a simmer and seasoned with just the right amount of salt, the chicken will be very juicy and it can be served just as it is, if so desired. One can taste the delicate flavors of the chicken, ham, and celery cabbage. This soup makes an excellent one-dish meal, and it is very easy to cook.

INGREDIENTS

1 chicken, about 4 pounds
$1/2$ pound Smithfield ham, trimmed and rinsed well but with the skin left on
1 pound celery cabbage, cut into 3 × 1-inch pieces
1 scallion
1 teaspoon salt

PREPARATION

Put the chicken and ham in a casserole. Add enough water to cover. Bring to a boil, then remove the scum from the top. Add the salt and scallion, cover the pot, and keep the heat low enough so that the water just simmers. Cook the chicken for 2 hours or until it is tender. Remove the scallion and skim the fat. Meanwhile, boil the celery cabbage in water until tender, add it to the chicken soup, and just heat through. Or leave the cut-up celery cabbage raw and add it directly to the soup. Cover and cook until very tender, about 15 minutes.

AT THE TABLE   Serve the chicken soup in a fire pot, a tureen, or a cook-and-serve casserole dish. The chicken is very tender, and it can be picked up easily with chopsticks or a fork. The ham should be sliced for easy serving. The slices may be put back in the soup or served separately on a plate as a side dish. For additional flavor, soy sauce dip may be served with the chicken. This dish goes well with rice, noodles, bread, or rolls.

Yield: 6 servings as a main course

YU NAI YA
Duck with Taro

Duck with taro is a famous moon festival dish of Ningpo during the eighth month of the lunar year. Perhaps it is because at that time the *yu nai* (taro) is in season. Taro is a starchy root vegetable with a slightly sweet taste. Duck is fatty but has tasty dark meat. When duck and taro are cooked together, the taro absorbs the rich duck gravy. This hearty dish is not only delicious but easy to prepare.

INGREDIENTS

1 4 to 5-pound duck
1 tablespoon coarse salt
2 scallions, cut into halves with 1 tablespoon minced scallion reserved for the garnish
2 1-inch slices gingerroot, crushed
1 teaspoon salt or to taste
1/4 cup dry sherry
1 pound small taros, preferably with pink tender tips

PREPARATION

Wash the duck, its giblets, and neck. Remove the skin from the neck and the fat from the duck. Wipe the duck dry inside and out. Rub the salt into the cavity of the duck and then all over the duck's exterior. Refrigerate overnight. Take the duck out of the refrigerator, rinse off the salt, and place the duck breast up in a casserole. Add the scallion halves, gingerroot, and about 8 cups of water. Bring the water to a boil. Remove the scum as it rises to the surface. Add salt and sherry, cover, and cook over low heat for 1½ hours. Discard the scallion and gingerroot, and skim off the fat. Up to this point, the dish can be prepared ahead of time.

Peel and discard the skin from the taros and cut them into chunks. Add the cut-up taros to the duck and continue cooking it at low heat 30 minutes or until the taros are very soft and the duck is tender. Add more salt to taste.

AT THE TABLE Serve in the fire pot or casserole, or you may remove the duck and broth to a large soup bowl. Garnish with the minced scallion over the duck before serving.

Yield: 6 servings as main dish

SZECHUAN NIU LOU MIEN
Szechuan Spicy Beef
with Noodles

The cut of shin beef that is used for stewing often has small amounts of sinew or tendon attached to the meat. Do not remove it, for this gelatinous substance is tender and good to eat when cooked, and it also makes the gravy richer. Tell your butcher not to cut it off nor discard it. Chinese cooks not only ask their butchers to save the sinew and tendon but may even buy an extra half pound to add to this stew and other soups. Sinew requires longer cooking. Blanch and boil it in water for about 1 hour before adding it to the meat.

INGREDIENTS

2 pounds shin beef (shank), cut into 1-inch chunks
6 tablespoons peanut or corn oil
1 teaspoon crushed red chili peppers
4 1-inch thin slices gingerroot
1 teaspoon Szechuan peppercorns
4 cloves garlic, crushed
2 star anise
4 tablespoons brown bean sauce
2 tablespoons dry sherry
4 tablespoons soy sauce
1 teaspoon sugar
6 cups hot water
1 pound fresh or dried noodles or linguine
2 scallions, finely chopped

PREPARATION   Over low heat, heat a heavy pot; add the oil, then the crushed chili pepper; stir-fry for 1 minute. Add the gingerroot, Szechuan peppercorns, garlic, star anise, and bean sauce. Continue to stir-fry until all the spices are well combined. Turn the heat to high, add the cut up beef and sinew if using, and stir-fry and sear in the hot sauce.

Add the sherry, soy sauce, sugar, and 6 cups hot water. Cover the pot and bring it to a rolling boil, then turn the heat down, let it simmer fast enough for the liquid to bubble. Cook the meat for 2 to 3 hours or until the sinew and meat are tender. Remove and discard the star anise and peppercorns that are floating on top. Taste the meat and adjust the seasonings. If it isn't spicy enough, add more hot pepper, or if not salty enough, add salt. The meat should be very tender and the gravy should be very spicy. This dish may be prepared ahead of time and reheated in a fire pot at the dinner table.

Cook the fresh noodles or linguine with boiling water in a large pot for 2 to 3 minutes. If dry noodles or linguine are used, cook for 8 to 10 minutes or according to the directions on the package. Drain and add 1 tablespoon oil to keep the noodles separate. Set in a serving bowl. Heat the prepared spicy beef in a fire pot or in a cook-and-serve casserole. Serve the noodles in individual bowls and spoon the beef and gravy over them. Garnish with the chopped scallion. The noodles and beef may be eaten with either chopsticks or a fork, but the gravy is eaten with a spoon.

Yield: 6 servings as a main dish

Variation:

$1/2$ pound of a parboiled leaf vegetable may be added to the fire pot when reheating the beef before serving. Stewing beef, brisket, or chuck may be used instead of shin beef. The dish may be thickened with 2 teaspoons cornstarch combined with 2 tablespoons water while it is cooking, if desired.

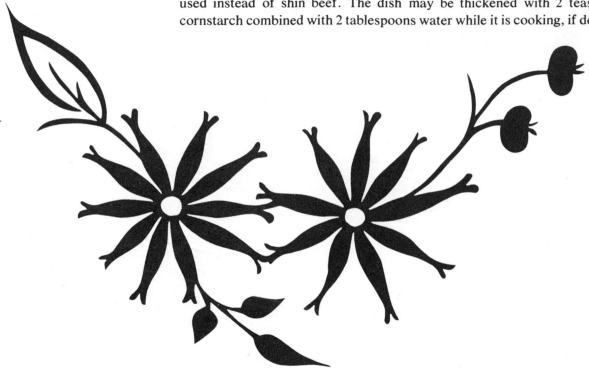

KUO PA T'ANG
Sizzling Rice Soup

The fire pot is the perfect utensil for cooking and serving this dish, since the soup consists of many different tasting ingredients. Best of all, it has "action" when served; the soup sizzles when hot rice patties are added just prior to serving. The aroma of the rice patties not only stimulates one's appetite, but the rice patties also give a little performance before you begin to eat your dinner.

INGREDIENTS

$^1/_2$ pound fresh shrimp, shelled, deveined, and diced

Marinade for shrimp:

1 teaspoon cornstarch
$^1/_2$ teaspoon salt
2 $^1/_2$-inch-thick boneless pork chops, thinly sliced into approximately 1 × 2-inch pieces

Marinade for pork:

2 teaspoons cornstarch
1 tablespoon water
1 tablespoon light soy sauce
1 tablespoon dry sherry

1 cup sliced fresh mushrooms or $^1/_2$ cup sliced canned mushrooms
$^1/_4$ cup sliced fresh or canned water chestnuts
$^1/_2$ cup frozen peas, thawed
6 cups chicken stock, page 8
1 teaspoon salt or to taste
$^1/_8$ teaspoon white pepper
8 pieces deep-fried rice patties, page 103, kept warm on a warming tray

PREPARATION	Combine the shrimp and pork in their respective marinades separately in small containers. Cover and refrigerate.
	Set the mushrooms, bamboo shoots, water chestnuts, and peas on a serving plate. All this can be done ahead of time if you wish to do so, but cover the plate with plastic wrap and refrigerate it until serving time.
AT THE TABLE	Preheat the oven to 450°. Take the containers of marinated shrimp and pork, the platter of prepared vegetables, and the fire pot to the dining table. Pour the chicken stock into the fire pot and bring it to a boil. Then add the meat and the vegetables. Stir to separate the meat slices and cook for 5 minutes. Add the shrimp and bring the mixture to a boil again. While the fire pot is cooking at the table, put the rice patties into the preheated oven and bake about 7 minutes or until very hot, but do not allow them to get more than lightly brown. Remove the patties from the oven and add them immediately to the boiling soup. Both the patties and the soup must be very hot when the patties are added in order for them to begin to sizzle. Serve the rice patties, seafood, meat, vegetables, and broth with a large spoon in individual rice bowls.

Yield: 4 servings as main dish; 8 servings as a soup

Note:

This dish can also be served in a cook-and-serve casserole. Cook the soup on the stove in the same manner. When the rice patties and soup are ready, bring them to the table. Add the patties so that the soup will sizzle in the presence of the diners.

P'AI KU T'ANG
Spareribs with Vegetables

Spareribs impart a special flavor to soups. However, since they require several hours of slow cooking, often they are cooked with vegetables that can be simmered for a long time and still hold their shape. Vegetables of this nature include white Chinese turnips, lotus root, and soy bean sprouts.

INGREDIENTS

1^1/$_2$ to 2 pounds spareribs
2   ^{1}/$_2$-inch pieces gingerroot
2   scallions
1^1/$_2$ teaspoons salt or to taste
Use any one of the following vegetables:
1   pound soybean sprouts (with roots removed, if desired), rinsed and drained
1   pound *lo po* (Chinese white turnips), peeled and cut into 1 × 1 × ^{1}/$_2$-inch slices
1   pound fresh lotus root, peeled and cut into 1 × 1 × ^{1}/$_4$-inch pieces, blanched in boiling water for 2 minutes

PREPARATION

Ask your butcher to chop the ribs across the bones into 1^1/$_2$-inch-long sections. Then cut between each rib. Bring 6 cups water to a boil, and add the gingerroot and scallions. Let the water boil for 5 minutes. Wash the cut-up spareribs in hot water and add to the soup. When the water begins to boil again, remove the scum as much as possible. If you are using lotus roots as a vegetable, add it to the soup at this time. Cover and let it simmer for 2 hours. If soybean sprouts or *lo po* are used, add them after the meat has been cooked for 1 hour. Continue to let soup simmer for 1 more hour. Remove and discard the scallions, skim off the fat, and add salt to taste.

AT THE TABLE Heat the prepared spareribs in a fire pot for about 10 minutes. Transfer to individual bowls. You may serve with light soy sauce as a dip.

Yield: 4 servings as a main course; 8 servings as a soup

Variations:

Pork shoulder, pork butt, or pork chops may be used instead of spareribs. Dried sliced lotus root can be used instead of fresh lotus root; soak 10 pieces in cold water overnight, drain, cut into 4 pieces, and cook in water for 1 hour before cooking with meat.

YEN TUN HSIEN
Fresh Pork and Corned Pork
with Bamboo Shoots

This dish traditionally is made with the combination of fresh and corned belly pork (bacon), cut up into 1-inch chunks with the skin left intact, and it is usually prepared when bamboo shoots are at their peak season. Since fresh pork and corned pork with skin are rarely available, this recipe calls for hocks instead. This dish tastes best when it is cooked a day ahead and reheated the next day in a *huo kuo* (fire pot).

INGREDIENTS

1 large corned or smoked pork hock, about 10 ounces
2 fresh pork hocks or 1 hock from the end of the shoulder, about $1\frac{1}{2}$ pounds
1 cup bamboo shoots cut up into 1-inch pieces, preferably from the bottom end of the shoot (tough part)
1 scallion
4 cups water or 1 can of chicken broth to which is added enough water to make 4 cups
2 pieces fresh-frozen bean curd sheets (optional), cut diagonally into 4 triangles (2 sheets make 8 triangles), see page 59
$\frac{1}{2}$ teaspoon salt or to taste

PREPARATION

Blanch fresh and corned pork hocks in boiling water for 5 minutes. If smoked hock is used, blanch the fresh hock first for 5 minutes, then remove it from the water and set aside. In the same water, boil the smoked hock for 15 minutes to remove the smoky flavor. Rinse the blanched hocks well to remove the scum and place them in a 2-quart pot. Add the 4 cups of water or broth and bring it to a boil. If there is any scum, remove it, and add the bamboo shoots and scallion. Cover, lower the heat, and let it simmer for about 3 hours or until it is very tender. The broth should be clear.

Beginning with the center corner, roll each softened bean curd triangle toward the wide side and tie it into a knot. Add the bean curd to the soup along with the salt and cook for 20 more minutes.

Yield: 4 servings as a main course

Variations:

A very lean slab of lightly smoked bacon may be used instead of corned pork or smoked pork hock. Cut the bacon into 1 × 2-inch pieces and blanch. Combine the smoked bacon with cut-up fresh bacon, boneless shoulder pork, or spare ribs instead of fresh pork hocks. Cook for 2 hours or until the meat is tender.

AT THE TABLE Reheat the soup in a fire pot for 10 minutes. Using a large spoon, ladle the meat and vegetables into individual rice bowls.

MIEN CHIN AND PAI YEH PAO
Stuffed Fried Wheat Gluten and Bean Curd Sheet Rolls

Not until recently were *pai yeh* (fresh-frozen bean curd sheets) and *mien chin* (wheat gluten) available in Chinese food markets in the United States. Before that *pai yeh* was not used in Chinese cooking here, because it cannot be made at home. But *mien chin* can be (see page 105). The process is by no means simple, but the efforts one puts into it are well worthwhile. It tastes so good, and it is a very nourishing food.

INGREDIENTS

Filling:

1 pound ground pork
1 teaspoon grated or minced gingerroot
1 tablespoon cornstarch
$^1/_2$ teaspoon salt
2 tablespoons light soy sauce
6 tablespoons canned chicken broth

Fire pot:

5 8 × 8-inch size *pai yeh* *(bean curd sheets)
$^1/_2$ teaspoon baking soda
2 teaspoons salt
20 *yu mien chin* (deep-fried wheat gluten), page 106
4 cups chicken stock, page 8, or pork meat stock, page 9, or canned chicken broth

* 59 *

Pai yeh comes in packages of 8 to 10 sheets. The extra sheets can be stored in the freezer.

PREPARATION Combine the filling ingredients. Using a spoon, stir in one direction until the ingredients are completely mixed and the ground meat holds together. Refrigerate. In a large pot, bring 2 quarts of water to a boil. Remove from heat and add the baking soda. Mix until soda dissolves. Stack the 5 bean curd sheets neatly and cut diagonally into 4 triangles (altogether there will be 20 triangles). Add them one by one to the hot water with soda. Make certain that all the bean curd triangles are submerged in the water. Gently stir to soak them evenly. Allow them to soak about 5 minutes. Soaking time depends on the thickness or freshness of the sheets. When they become creamy white, transfer them to a container of cold water. Leave the sheets soaking and set aside. If the bean curd triangles are too soft, they may be hardened by soaking them in a salt solution of 2 teaspoons salt in 4 cups cold water.

Prepared fried wheat gluten tends to be greasy and consequently needs to be soaked in water. Put it in a bowl, pour boiling water over it, and, using a spoon, stir and squeeze the fried wheat gluten against the side of the bowl. Let it soak for 5 minutes. Drain off the hot water and rinse it again in warm water. Squeeze each wheat gluten piece dry. Now the prepared wheat gluten is ready to be filled. Homemade fried wheat gluten may be stuffed without preparation.

To wrap the filling with the bean curd triangles:

Take a bean curd triangle from the soaking water. Lay it flat on a plate and fill it with 1 tablespoon of meat filling. Shape it into a 3-inch-long sausagelike form and lay it along the wide side of the triangle. Fold the two short corners to cover the filling and roll toward the center corner into a bundle like an egg roll. This is called a bean curd sheet roll. Line the bean curd rolls concentrically in an 8-inch-diameter greased shallow bowl.

To stuff the fried wheat gluten:

Make a hole in each fried wheat gluten and stuff each piece with 1 tablespoon of the remaining filling. Place on top of the bean curd rolls. Cover with a piece of plastic wrap. Steam the filled fried wheat gluten and bean curd rolls over medium heat for 15 minutes. This dish can be cooked ahead of time up until this point.

AT THE TABLE

Before serving, invert the steamed wheat gluten and bean curd rolls into a large, deep, and round cook-and-serve casserole, a chafing dish, or fire pot. Add the cold stock slowly around the bowl so that the bean curd rolls will retain their shape. Add salt to taste; remove the mold bowl and slowly bring the stock to a boil. Cook for 15 minutes.

Yield: 6 servings as a main course; 10 servings as a soup

Variations:

If less meat is desired, use ½ recipe of the meat filling for the bean curd rolls. Add softened fried wheat gluten over the bean curd rolls and steam. They will be just as delicious. Add ½ pound of celery cabbage heart and cook it until it is tender. Place it over the wheat gluten before steaming.

TAN CHUEN FEN SZE T'ANG
Pork Egg Rolls with
Cellophane Noodles
INGREDIENTS

Filling:

1/2 pound finely ground pork, about 1 cup
1   large egg, beaten*
1/2 tablespoon cornstarch
1/2 teaspoon salt
1   tablespoon soy sauce
4   tablespoons canned chicken broth

Egg sheets:

4   eggs
1/4 teaspoon salt
3   teaspoons peanut or corn oil

Fire Pot:

2   ounces cellophane noodles, soaked in boiling water for 20 minutes
1/2   pound spinach, parboiled
4   cups chicken stock, page 8
1 1/2 teaspoons salt or to taste
1/8   teaspoon white pepper

*Use 1/2 the egg for the filling and reserve 1/2 the egg to combine with the egg sheet.

PREPARATION   Using ½ of the beaten egg, combine with the filling ingredients in a mixing bowl. Mix and stir in one direction until the meat holds together and becomes like a paste. Set aside. For the egg sheets, add the remaining ½ beaten egg to the other eggs, then beat the eggs thoroughly with the salt and 1 teaspoon oil.

COOKING   To make an 8-inch skillet nonsticking, treat it by heating the pan until very hot. Add oil to coat the entire pan, then pour out the excess oil. Allow it to cool completely. Turn the heat to low and let the pan get hot. Add ¼ of the beaten eggs to the pan and swirl around to make a 7-inch-diameter egg sheet. Have the heat high enough so that the underside browns slightly, but before the eggs are completely set, remove the sheet from the pan. Add more oil as necessary, and with the remaining egg mixture make three more egg sheets. Divide the meat filling into four portions. Using a sandwich spreader, spread a portion of filling thinly and evenly over each egg sheet. Roll each egg sheet with the filling tightly and press to seal. Place the finished pork egg rolls on a plate and steam them in a steamer over low heat for 10 minutes. Turn off the heat and allow them to remain in the steamer for 5 minutes. Up to this point, the pork egg rolls may be prepared in advance. Cover and keep in the refrigerator. Cut the cold egg rolls in diagonal slices to make them more interesting looking.

AT THE TABLE Drain the cellophane noodles and place them on a serving dish along with the parboiled spinach. Pour the chicken stock into a fire pot or a cook-and-serve casserole. Turn the heat on and bring the stock to a boil. Add the salt and cellophane noodles and let the ingredients boil for 2 or 3 minutes. Add the spinach and the pork egg roll slices and allow the soup to heat through. Add the white pepper and serve hot. Use chopsticks or a fork to remove the noodles and vegetables first, then ladle out the pork egg roll slices and soup into the individual rice bowls or soup plates.

Yield: 4 servings as a main course

Variations:

Ground beef or veal may be used instead of pork. Celery cabbage may be used instead of spinach.

Note:

Pork egg rolls may be served as a main dish when cooked together with peas or celery cabbage and $1/2$ chicken broth. They are also good as appetizers and may be served either hot or cold.

BO TS'AI JOU YUAN T'ANG
Meatballs with Spinach Soup

INGREDIENTS

Meatballs:

$1/2$ pound finely chopped pork, about 1 cup
$1/2$ tablespoon peanut or corn oil
$1/2$ teaspoon salt
1 tablespoon light soy sauce
3 tablespoons canned chicken broth

Fire Pot:

4 cups chicken stock, page 8, or meat stock, page 9, or 4 cups water with $1/4$ teaspoon monosodium glutamate
2 ounces cellophane noodles, soaked in boiling water for 20 minutes
2 cups tender spinach leaves or watercress
1 teaspoon salt or to taste
$1/8$ teaspoon white pepper

PREPARATION　　　Combine the ground pork with the seasonings. Stir in one direction until the meat holds together and has a slight resistance. In a large pot, bring 4 cups stock or water to a boil. Shape the meat into 1-inch balls and, as you make them, drop them into the gently boiling liquid. Let them simmer for 5 minutes. Lift the balls from the pot and cool them in a bowl of cold water. When cool, discard the water. Or if the stock is not used, after cooking in the water, just leave the meatballs in the cooking water. Add ¼ teaspoon monosodium glutamate to finish cooking the dish, and then add the remaining ingredients. Serve hot.

AT THE TABLE　　　In a fire pot, or cook-and-serve casserole, add the stock, meatballs, and drained cellophane noodles. Bring to a boil and cook for 2 minutes. Add the salt and pepper and the spinach or watercress. Press the vegetable down into the broth and continue to cook until it wilts. Serve hot.

Yield: 4 servings as a main course; 8 servings as a soup

Variations:

If you like a hot, peppery taste, add 2 tablespoons shredded Szechuan *cha ts'ai* (Szechuan preserved vegetable). Ground beef or veal may be used instead of pork. If shrimp balls (page 75) are added, this fire pot becomes an elegant dish to serve to guests.

YU TOU FU CH'IEN JOU
Fried Bean Curd Stuffed with Pork

INGREDIENTS: **Filling:**

$^1/_2$ pound ground pork
$^1/_4$ teaspoon salt
$^1/_2$ tablespoon cornstarch
1   tablespoon soy sauce
3   tablespoons canned chicken broth

$^1/_2$ pound fried bean curd, about 14 1$^1/_2$-inch-square pieces
$^1/_2$ teaspoon baking soda
$^1/_2$ tablespoon soy sauce
$^1/_2$ teaspoon sugar
1   cup canned chicken broth or enough to cover the bean curd

Fire Pot:

4   cups chicken stock, page 8
2   ounces cellophane noodles, soaked in boiling water until cool
1   teaspoon salt
$^1/_8$ teaspoon white pepper
1   teaspoon sesame oil

PREPARATION   Combine the filling ingredients in a mixing bowl. Stir the mixture in one direction until it holds together. Refrigerate.

In a saucepan, add 4 cups water and bring to a boil. Add the baking soda, mix well, and remove from heat. Add the fried bean curd to the pan of water and weigh them down with a small plate so that they are submerged under the water. Let soak for 10 minutes. Rinse the fried bean curd thoroughly and squeeze out all the water.

Divide the ground meat mixture into 14 portions. Make a slit into each of the bean curd squares and stuff each piece with a portion of the meat filling. Arrange the stuffed bean curd with the open sides up in one layer in a pot just large enough to hold all the pieces. Add the soy sauce, sugar, and broth. If the pot is too large there will not be enough liquid to cover; add a little water if necessary. The stuffed bean curd should be covered with liquid while cooking.

COOKING   Slowly bring the pot of stuffed bean curd to a boil and let it cook over low heat for 30 minutes. Turn the stuffed bean curd once after cooking. Serve hot and use the stuffed bean curd as a major ingredient in the fire pot, or this dish can be cooked ahead of time and be reheated. The cooked stuffed bean curd can be refrigerated for 2 to 3 days.

AT THE TABLE   Cut the cold stuffed bean curd pieces into halves and add them to the fire pot with the stock. Heat the pot at the dining table. Add the cellophane noodles and season with salt and pepper. Let the fire pot ingredients cook for 10 minutes. Add a few drops of sesame oil just before serving. Using chopsticks or a fork, serve the stuffed bean curds and the cellophane noodles into individual rice bowls or soup plates, then ladle out the broth.

Yield: 4 servings as a main course; 8 servings as a soup

NIANG TOU FU
Fresh Bean Curd Stuffed with Shrimp and Pork

INGREDIENTS

6 3 × 3 × 1-inch pieces fresh firm bean curd

Filling:

$1/2$ pound raw shrimp, shelled and deveined
$1/4$ pound ground pork, about $1/2$ cup (ground from boneless shoulder of pork or pork chops)
$1/2$ teaspoon salt
$1/8$ teaspoon white pepper
1 tablespoon light soy sauce
1 tablespoon dry sherry
2 teaspoons sesame oil

3 tablespoons peanut or corn oil
1 teaspoon salt
$1/2$ teaspoon sugar
$1/8$ teaspoon white pepper
1 tablespoon soy sauce
$1/4$ cup chicken broth

Fire Pot:

6 cups pork stock, page 9, or chicken stock, page 8
2 ounces cellophane noodles, soaked in boiling water for 20 minutes
$1/2$ pound spinach or 1 bunch watercress

PREPARATION   Cut each bean curd piece diagonally into 4 triangular pieces. Using a paring knife, scoop out part of the bean curd to make it hollow so that the center can be filled.

Shrimp and meat filling:

Chop the shrimp and mix with the ground pork and seasonings to form a soft paste. If the consistency is too dry, add a little of the scooped-out bean curd. Take a heaping teaspoon of the filling and stuff into the hollowed out bean curd triangles. Repeat until all 24 pieces are filled.

COOKING   Heat a large frying pan. Add the oil and place each piece of stuffed bean curd filling-side down in the pan. Fry them for 2 minutes and then turn them over and fry the other side for another minute. Add the salt, sugar, pepper, soy sauce, and, lastly, the broth. Cover and cook for 3 minutes over medium heat. The dish can be served as it is, or the bean curd can be made ahead of time and used as the principal ingredient for a fire pot soup.

AT THE TABLE   For the fire pot, add the stuffed bean curd pieces to the pot along with the stock. Add the cellophane noodles and spinach or watercress. Bring to a boil and let it cook 10 minutes. With chopsticks or a fork remove the bean curd pieces and cellophane noodles to individual rice bowls or soup plates. Ladle out the vegetables and broth.

Yield: 4 servings as a main dish with or without soup

Contemporary Fire Pots
for Soups or Light Meals

HSIEH JOU CHEN CHU T'ANG
Velvet Crab Meat and Corn Soup

INGREDIENTS

3 egg whites
2 tablespoons minced cooked Smithfield ham
1 tablespoon cornstarch combined with 1/4 cup water
4 cups chicken stock, page 8
1 8 3/4-ounce can cream of corn
1 teaspoon salt or to taste
1 cup crab meat, broken into 1-inch pieces
1/8 teaspoon white pepper

PREPARATION

Beat the egg whites until fluffy. Set aside with the minced ham and cornstarch in water. In the fire pot add the chicken stock, creamed corn, and salt. Up to this point the dish may be prepared ahead of time.

AT THE TABLE

Just before serving, bring the soup to a rolling boil. Stir the cornstarch and water well and pour slowly into the broth. Keep simmering. Add the crab meat and white pepper and gently stir in the beaten egg whites. Top with the minced ham. Serve immediately. If the egg whites are overcooked they will lose their velvety texture.

Yield: 6 servings as a soup

SUAN LA HSIA MI FEN SZU
Hot and Sour Shrimp with
Cellophane Noodles

Good cellophane noodles will not get soggy even when they are overcooked, and fortunately most of them on the market are of good quality. This light lunch dish is especially easy to prepare.

INGREDIENTS

4 ounces *fen szu* (cellophane noodles)
40 dried medium shrimps, $1/2$ inch in diameter (if larger ones are used, break them in halves and use 20)
2 tablespoons oil
2 tablespoons dry sherry
2 tablespoons soy sauce
4 cups boiling water
$1/8$ teaspoon monosodium glutamate (optional)
$1/4$ teaspoon white pepper
2 tablespoons cider vinegar
  Salt (optional)
1 tablespoon sesame oil
1 tablespoon finely chopped scallion

PREPARATION

Soak the cellophane noodles in 1 quart boiling water and let them remain in the water until it cools down. Then drain off the excess water.

In a wok, stir fry the dried shrimp in the oil over low heat for 2 minutes. Add the sherry and cover for 5 seconds. To a fire pot or cook-and-serve casserole, add the cellophane noodles, soy sauce, 4 cups boiling water, and monosodium glutamate, if you are using it. Add the shrimp and sherry sauce. Turn the heat to high and bring the soup to a boil. Let it cook for 5 minutes. Add the white pepper and cider vinegar. The saltiness of the dried shrimp varies, so taste the dish before adding any salt and adjust according to your taste. Lastly, add the sesame oil and chopped scallion.

Using chopsticks, serve the cellophane noodles into individual bowls first, then ladle the soup into each bowl. Serve with chopsticks and soup spoons.

Yield: 4 servings as a light meal; 8 servings as a soup

HSIA CHIU T'ANG
Shrimp Ball Soup

**INGREDIENTS FOR
SHRIMP BALLS**

2   egg whites
2   ounces cooked pork fat, preserved ham fat, or blanched fatty bacon
4   water chestnuts (optional)
1   pound raw shrimp, shelled and deveined
1   tablespoon cornstarch
$1^1/_2$ teaspoons salt
$^1/_8$ teaspoon white pepper
1   tablespoon dry sherry

PREPARATION

If a food processor is available, blend the egg whites, pork fat, and water chestnuts first. Then add the shrimp and the remaining ingredients and blend until the mixture holds together.

If a meat grinder is used, beat the egg whites separately until foamy. Grind the shrimp, pork fat, and water chestnuts. Combine with the remaining ingredients and egg whites.

If a cleaver is used, chop the shrimp very fine and make the mixture in the same manner as with the meat grinder.

Put 4 cups of cold water in a saucepan. With your left hand, take a handful of the shrimp paste and squeeze your fingers into a fist, forcing the paste up between your thumb and forefinger, forming a ball about the size of a walnut. With your right hand, take a tablespoon that has been dipped into the cold water (to prevent sticking) and scoop up the shrimp ball and drop it into the cold water. When all the shrimp paste is used, place the pot with the raw shrimp balls over medium heat. When the water just begins to boil, lower the heat and let it simmer for 1 minute. Transfer the shrimp balls into another container of cold water to cool them. When they are cooled, drain off the water. If the shrimp balls are not immediately used, they may be kept in cold water in a covered container and stored in the refrigerator up to 2 days.

Yield: 20 to 24 shrimp balls

INGREDIENTS FOR SOUP

12 dried Chinese mushrooms
12 1 × 2 × 1^1/$_8$-inch slices bamboo shoots
4 cups chicken stock, page 8
   Shrimp balls (see recipe above)
2 teaspoons finely chopped scallion
1 teaspoon salt
^{1}/$_8$ teaspoon white pepper
2 teaspoons fish sauce or light soy sauce

PREPARATION

Wash and soak the mushrooms in warm water for 30 minutes. Remove and discard the stems. If the mushrooms are large, cut them into two pieces. Set them aside with the bamboo shoots.

AT THE TABLE In a fire pot, add the chicken stock, shrimp balls, mushrooms, and bamboo shoots. Slowly bring to a boil, then turn the heat low and let it simmer for 5 minutes. Add the scallion, salt, white pepper, and fish sauce or light soy sauce. Serve hot.

Yield: 6 servings as a soup

Variation:

The ingredients used in meat balls with spinach soup (page 65) can be added to the ingredients in this fire pot. Then this dish can be served as a main course for 6 people.

YÜ YÜAN T'ANG
Fish Ball Soup

INGREDIENTS

³/₄ pound fillet of pike, sea bass, gray sole, or other white fish
¹/₂ cup cold water

Seasoning:

1   ¹/₂-inch chunk gingerroot
1¹/₂ teaspoons salt
¹/₄ teaspoon sugar
¹/₄ teaspoon monosodium glutamate
1   tablespoon cornstarch
1   tablespoon peanut or corn oil
2   egg whites

1   quart cold water
4   cups clear chicken stock, page 8
1   teaspoon finely chopped scallion
1   tablespoon fish sauce
¹/₂ teaspoon salt or to taste
¹/₈ teaspoon white pepper

PREPARATION

Cut the fish into small chunks. Set aside the ¹/₂ cup cold water. Using a garlic press, extract the juice from the ginger and discard the pulp. Add the remaining seasoning ingredients to the ginger juice. Using a food processor, grind the fish for 30 seconds, adding the cold water, $1/2$ tablespoon at a time. Add the seasoning ingredients, grind; add the egg whites last and grind some more. The fish paste will gradually become stiffer.

Pour 1 quart cold water into a saucepan. With your left hand, take a handful of the fish paste and squeeze your fingers into a fist, forcing the paste up between your thumb and forefinger, forming a ball about the size of the walnut. With your right hand, dip a small spoon into the cold water (to prevent sticking), then use the spoon to scoop up the fish ball from your left hand. Drop the ball into the cold water. Repeat until you have made and dropped all the fish balls into the water. Turn the heat to medium-low, and slowly bring to a boil. The fish balls are ready to be removed from the pot when they float to the surface. Transfer the fish balls into a pot of cold water to cool. They may be stored in a container with water to cover. Cover the container and refrigerate until cooking time or as long as 2 days.

AT THE TABLE   Pour the chicken stock into a fire pot. Drain fish balls and add them to the cold broth. Slowly bring to a boil, lower the heat, and let simmer for 5 minutes. Add the chopped scallion, fish sauce, salt, and white pepper just before serving. Serve hot.

Yield: 6 servings as soup

Variations:

Sliced cooked Smithfield ham, bamboo shoots, and mushrooms may be added to the soup.

YANG JOU T'ANG CH'UAN YÜ P'IEN
Fillet of Sole with Lamb Broth

There is no exact translation in English for the word *hsien*. *Hsien* can be best described as a pleasant reaction of the taste buds when eating food seasoned with a small amount of monosodium glutamate. When this salt is added to food, it tends to provide a sweet taste. And this is why Hsiang Ju Lin and Tsuifeng Lin, in their book *Chinese Gastronomy,* describe the word *hsien* as sweet. *Hsien,* when written in Chinese, consists of the combination of two characters: "fish" and "lamb." The following soup is made of fish fillet and lamb broth, which makes it "sweet" and good tasting or *hsien*.

INGREDIENTS

1 fillet of gray sole, about 1/2 pound
1/2 teaspoon salt
1 teaspoon cornstarch
6 cups lamb stock, page 8
1 teaspoon salt or to taste

Garnish:

2 teaspoons dry sherry
1/4 teaspoon white pepper
1 teaspoon sesame oil
1/4 cup coriander leaves

PREPARATION   Cut the fillet lengthwise into 2 strips. Remove any bones found in the center. Cut each half fillet at a slight angle to the grain into $1/4$-inch-thick slices. In a bowl, mix the fish slices well with the salt and cornstarch. Spread the fish slices on a plate and cover with plastic wrap and refrigerate.

AT THE TABLE   Add the lamb broth to the fire pot and set it on the dining table. Before serving, bring the lamb stock to a boil and add the salt. Slide the fish fillet slices from the plate into the broth and gently stir to separate the slices. Cook for a minute or two and top with the garnish ingredients. Serve hot in individual rice bowls.

Yield: 6 to 8 servings as a soup

Variations:

Instead of gray sole, fillet of scrod or yellow pike may be used. Instead of lamb stock, chicken stock may be used.

HUANG YU KENG
Ningpo Fish Chowder

INGREDIENTS

$^1/_2$ pound fillet of whiting or other white fish (reserve the fish heads and bones)

2 egg whites

1 teaspoon salt

$^1/_4$ cup finely shredded bamboo shoots

$^1/_2$ cup finely chopped *hsüeh li hung* (preserved red-in-snow)

2 tablespoons finely chopped coriander leaves

3 cups fish stock made from the reserved fish head and bones, to which a pinch of monosodium glutamate has been added, or 1 $13^3/_4$-ounce can chicken broth, diluted with enough water to make 3 cups

$1^1/_2$ tablespoons cornstarch combined with 3 tablespoons water

2 teaspoons sesame oil

$^1/_8$ teaspoon white pepper

PREPARATION

Cut the fillet into $^1/_4$-inch cubes and add $^1/_2$ of one egg white to the fish along with $^1/_2$ teaspoon salt and mix very well. Reserve the remaining $1^1/_2$ egg whites to be used later. Set in the refrigerator. Set the shredded bamboo shoots, chopped preserved red-in-snow, and chopped coriander leaves on one plate.

COOKING Add the 3 cups broth to a fire pot or a cook-and-serve casserole. Bring to a boil and add the salt, bamboo shoots, and preserved red-in-snow. Cook for 2 minutes. Stir the cornstarch and water well and slowly add to the soup. Add the fillet. Bring to a boil again, then lower the heat. Beat the remaining egg whites until foamy and slightly fluffy. Slowly add to the soup. Gently stir once. Turn off heat or remove casserole from heat. Garnish with chopped coriander and sesame oil. Season with the white pepper. Serve hot.

Yield: 6 servings as a soup

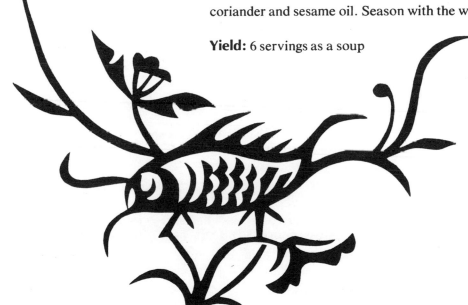

YÜ TU T'ANG
Fish Maw Soup

Fish maw is the air bladder of a large fish. If it is purchased dried, after soaking it will feel smooth. Its rubbery and spongy texture enables it to soak up and absorb the rich gravy in which it is usually cooked. Fish maw can be made puffy by deep frying in oil. It can also be purchased already puffed up; this is done by cooking it in hot sand. Although fish maw is spongy, it also has a slightly crispy texture. It is always cooked in concentrated meat and chicken stock. Since the fish maw is actually tasteless, it is cooked in a rich gravylike broth, which it absorbs. When you bite into a piece of fish maw, you taste the good gravy and feel its unique texture.

INGREDIENTS

4   medium dried mushrooms
2   ounces puffed fish maw
1   $1/2$-inch piece fresh gingerroot, crushed
1   tablespoon dry sherry
$1/4$ teaspoon white pepper
4   cups rich chicken and meat stock, page 9
$1/2$ cup thinly sliced ($1 \times 2 \times 1/8$-inch) bamboo shoots
10 fresh snow pea pods, ends and strings removed, cut in halves
$1/2$ cup thinly sliced ($1 \times 2 \times 1/8$-inch) cooked Smithfield ham
1   teaspoon salt or to taste

PREPARATION   Wash and soak the mushrooms in $1/2$ cup warm water for 30 minutes. Drain. Remove and discard the mushroom stems and cut each mushroom into 4 pieces. Set aside on a plate.

Soak the fish maw in 1 quart of cold water for 30 minutes; use a plate to weigh down the fish maw while soaking.

In a pot bring the fish maw and soaking water to a boil. Add the gingerroot, sherry, and pepper. Remove from the heat and, using a large spoon, stir the maw around several times. Allow it to cool, and then with your hand, squeeze the maw in the warm water 2 or 3 times to rinse out the fish flavor. Squeeze out all the water and cut the maw into $1/2 \times 1^{1}/_{2}$-inch strips. You should have about 2 cups.

AT THE TABLE   Heat the rich stock in a fire pot or saucepan and add the fish maw, bamboo shoots, and mushrooms. Bring to a boil, then simmer for 15 minutes. Add the snow pea pods and ham, then add the salt. Mix well and serve hot.

Yield: 6 to 8 servings as a soup

CHI YI T'ANG
Gingerroot Chicken Wing Soup

With 8 to 16 chicken wings, you can make the following two soups, one simple, the other fancy, and both delicious.

INGREDIENTS

1 tablespoon peanut or corn oil
4 1/2-inch slices of gingerroot, peeled
8 chicken wings, cut into 2 sections, with the wing tips and any attached extra skin discarded
1/4 cup dry sherry
5 cups boiling water
1 scallion
2 teaspoons salt or to taste

PREPARATION

Heat a wok, add the oil and gingerroot, and stir fry for 1 minute. Add the cut-up chicken wing sections. Stir constantly and fry until they begin to brown. Add the sherry, stir, then cover immediately, and let them sizzle for a few seconds. Remove to a fire pot, a cook-and-serve casserole, or a heavy saucepan. Add the boiling water, scallion, and salt. Bring the soup to a boil, lower the heat, cover, and let the soup simmer for 30 minutes or until the chicken wings are tender. Remove the scallion and skim off the fat. The gingerroot pieces retain their flavor, and they may be left in the soup.

Yield: 8 servings as a soup

Variations:

8 dried mushrooms, rinsed and soaked for 1/2 hour, may be added to the soup. For a richer soup, chicken stock may be used instead of water.

LUNG CH'UAN FENG YI T'ANG

Fancy Stuffed Chicken Wing Soup

INGREDIENTS   16 middle sections of 16 chicken wings*

Filling:

4   large dried mushrooms, soaked in 1 cup warm water for 30 minutes
16   2 × ¼ × ⅛-inch strips Smithfield ham (1 large thin slice either cooked or raw ham)
16   2 × ¼ × ⅛-inch strips bamboo shoots

PREPARATION   The bones of the midsections of the chicken wings are easily removed by chopping off the enlarged part of each end, then pushing out the two straight bones against a table top. Set aside. Cut each mushroom into four strips approximately the same size as the ham and bamboo shoot strips. If there is any mushroom soaking water left, discard the sediment and add to the soup in place of water. Take one strip of each of the above three ingredients and thread them into the center of each wing section where the bones were removed. Cook the soup with the stuffed chicken wing sections as for gingerroot chicken wing soup (p. 86).

Yield: 8 servings

*The tips may be used for stock, and the thick sections of the wings may be used for gingerroot chicken wing soup.

TS'AI HSIN CHI T'ANG
Celery Cabbage with Clear Chicken Broth

There is a story that goes with this dish about a Chinese general who asked his cook to prepare the same chicken dish daily. One day the cook altered the dish, serving the general vegetables in a clear chicken broth. Although the dish was exquisitely prepared, the general still asked where his chicken was. He didn't realize that all that year while he had been eating the chicken, the cook was having the best part of the dish: the clear chicken broth.

INGREDIENTS

1   1-pound heart of celery cabbage, about 3 inches round and 5 inches long, or 2 smaller hearts of celery cabbage
4   cups homemade clear chicken stock, page 8
12   2 × 1 × ⅛-inch slices cooked Smithfield ham
     Salt and white pepper to taste
2   tablespoons *shao-hsin* rice wine or dry sherry

PREPARATION

Bring 2 quarts of water to a boil. Split the celery cabbage heart lengthwise in two and drop into the boiling water. Cook without covering over medium-high heat for approximately 10 minutes or until almost tender. Rinse and soak in cold water until completely cold. Drain.

AT THE TABLE

In a fire pot, add the drained cabbage and chicken stock. Add the ham and bring the soup to a boil. Add salt and pepper to taste. Add the wine and serve hot.

Yield: 6 servings as a soup

SUAN LA NIU JOU T'ANG
Hot and Sour Beef Soup

INGREDIENTS

¹/₂ pound flank steak

Marinade:

1   tablespoon cornstarch
1   tablespoon water
1¹/₂ tablespoons soy sauce
¹/₂ tablespoon oil

20   tiger lily buds
¹/₄ cup dried tree ears
1   4 × 4 × 1¹/₂-inch piece fresh tender bean curd
1¹/₄ teaspoons salt
1   large egg, well beaten
2   teaspoons sesame oil
2   teaspoons minced scallion
4   cups beef stock, page 9, or chicken stock, page 8
1   tablespoon soy sauce
¹/₄ teaspoon white pepper
2   tablespoons cider vinegar
2   tablespoons cornstarch, combined with ¹/₄ cup cold water

PREPARATION

Slice the flank steak into 1 × 1¹/₂ × ¹/₄-inch pieces. Combine with the marinade ingredients and mix well. Refrigerate for 30 minutes. Soak the tiger lily buds and tree ears in separate bowls of water. Discard the hard ends of the lily buds, if there are any. Tie each bud in a knot and set aside. Rinse the tree ears several times, drain off water, and squeeze and break into small pieces if large. You should now have about 1 cup. Set aside with the lily buds.

Handle the tender bean curd gently, and slice it into $1 \times 2 \times 1/4$-inch pieces. Sprinkle with $1/4$ teaspoon salt and set aside for 10 minutes.

Drop the marinated beef in a pot of boiling water, stir to separate the slices, and cook until the meat has changed color. Drain the cooled beef and set aside. Season the beaten egg with the sesame oil and minced scallion and set aside. Add the stock to a fire pot or a cook-and-serve casserole. Add the remaining $1/4$ teaspoon salt, soy sauce, white pepper, cider vinegar, lily buds, and tree ears. This soup can be prepared ahead of time up to this point and cooked later.

AT THE TABLE   Just a few minutes before serving, drain off the excess water from the bean curd pieces and add them to the soup. Slowly bring the soup to a boil. To thicken the soup, mix the cornstarch well in the water and add it gradually to the soup while stirring. When the soup has thickened, add the blanched beef and cook until it begins to boil again. Slowly add the seasoned beaten egg, turn off the heat, and gently stir only once, allowing the egg to cook for half a minute, then serve at once.

Yield: 4 servings as a light meal with plain rice; 8 servings as soup

Variations:

1 chicken breast or $1/2$ pound lean pork may be used instead of beef.

NIU JOU T'ANG
Beef with Mixed Vegetables Soup

INGREDIENTS

2 pounds beef neck bones, with meat attached
2 tablespoons peanut or corn oil
1 medium onion, quartered
1 cup chopped carrots
1 cup chopped celery
2 cups chopped cabbage
4 cups boiling water
1 1-inch slice gingerroot, crushed
  Salt and pepper to taste
  Pinch monosodium glutamate (optional)

PREPARATION

Ask your butcher to chop each neck bone into 4 or 5 irregular 2-inch pieces. In a large saucepan, parboil the neck bones for 5 minutes. Discard the water and rinse the neck bones.

Heat the same saucepan. Add the oil and stir-fry the onion until it is transparent. Add the carrots, stir and cook together for 2 minutes. Then add the celery and cabbage and continue to stir-fry a couple minutes longer. Put the neck bones back in the pan, add the 4 cups of boiling water and allow it to return to a boil. Remove the scum, add the gingerroot, and cover. Lower the heat and let it simmer for 2 to 3 hours or until the meat on the bone can be picked off with either chopsticks or a fork. Either remove and discard the bones, or you may keep them and serve them with the soup. Season the soup with salt and pepper. Taste it, and add a pinch of monosodium glutamate if needed.

AT THE TABLE Carefully transfer the contents of the soup to a fire pot or cook-and-serve casserole. Bring to a boil, cook for 1 minute, and then serve in individual rice bowls. To make this soup into a light meal, any of the following may be served with the soup: plain hot rice; crusty bread, such as Italian bread; silver needle noodles (page 107); or very thin spaghetti, cooked. Also, 1/2 pound uncooked rice sticks or cooked egg noodles may be added directly to the boiling soup. Bring back to a boil and cook for 1 minute. Serve in large bowls.

Yield: 4 servings as a light meal

Variations:

Ox tail, shin, chuck, or pork neck bones may be used instead of beef neck bones. Green beans, beets, cucumber, collard greens, tomatoes, and soy bean sprouts can be cooked with pork neck bones instead of the onion, carrots, celery, and cabbage.

HUANG KUA JOU P'IEN T'ANG
Pork and Cucumber Ring Soup

INGREDIENTS

$^1/_2$ pound boneless pork, cut from the hip, or center-cut chops

Marinade:

1 tablespoon light soy sauce or $^1/_2$ teaspoon salt
1$^1/_2$ tablespoons cornstarch
2 tablespoons water

1 large cucumber
6 to 8 cups chicken stock, page 8, or pork stock, page 9, seasoned with salt to taste

PREPARATION

Cut the pork into $2 \times 1 \times ^1/_8$-inch slices, and put them in a bowl. Add the marinade ingredients and mix. If the meat seems dry, add a little more water. Mix well to make sure all the meat slices are well coated with the marinade. Refrigerate for at least 30 minutes.

Peel the cucumber and cut it crosswise into 1-inch-thick sections. Remove the seeds in the center and slice the centerless sections into $^1/_8$-inch-thick ring-shaped slices. Or for an easier way of removing the seeds, the cucumber may be cut lengthwise. Scrape out the seeds in the center, then cut into thin crescent-shaped slices. Store the cucumber slices in a covered container in the refrigerator until just before serving time.

Blanch the marinated meat slices by adding them to a saucepan containing 4 cups of boiling water. Stir the meat slices gently, and keep the heat on just until the meat slices separate. Turn off the heat and drain. Cool the blanched meat by dropping the pieces into a container with 4 cups of cold water. Drain immediately. The meat can be prepared up to this stage several hours ahead of serving time and refrigerated until you are ready to finish cooking.

AT THE TABLE Add the prepared stock to the fire pot, bring it to a boil, then keep it at a simmer. Just before serving, add the blanched meat and cucumber rings to the soup and cook until the stock begins to boil. Serve immediately in individual rice bowls.

Yield: 6 to 8 servings as a soup

Variations:

Boneless veal or 1 small chicken breast cut into $2 \times 1 \times 1/8$-inch slices may be used instead of pork. To use the chicken breast, marinate the slices with $1/2$ teaspoon salt, $1^1/2$ tablespoons cornstarch, 2 tablespoons water, and $1/8$ teaspoon monosodium glutamate. Blanch the chicken as with the pork, then add it to the soup.

HUO T'UI TUNG KUA T'ANG

Ham in Winter Melon Soup

INGREDIENTS

3   thin slices cooked Smithfield ham, about $1/4$ pound
$1^1/_2$ pounds winter melon
6   cups chicken stock, page 8
$1/_2$ teaspoon salt or to taste

PREPARATION

Cut the ham slices into 1×2-inch pieces, and set aside. Winter melons come in large and varied sizes. It is sold by weight in wedges. The width of the wedges will vary according to the size of the melon. $1^1/_2$ pounds of winter melon may be 1 to 2 inches wide depending on the length of each wedge. It is impossible to give precise directions as to how to cut the melon into slices, since the size of the wedges varies so much. Cut the winter melon wedge into manageable pieces. Remove the skin, seeds, and pith. Rinse and boil the melon in water for about 10 minutes or until just soft. When it is cool enough to handle, you can begin to cut it into slices. Use your own good judgment and cut the melon into approximately $2 \times 1^1/_2 \times 1/_4$-inch-thick slices. Each slice should be cut so that it includes one side where the skin was and one side of inner flesh. Make a deep slit where formerly the seeds were held, leaving the skin side attached so that the ham slices may be sandwiched within the melon and the slice remains intact.

As a mold, use a shallow bowl just large enough to hold the melon sandwiches. Arrange them with the skin sides down in an overlapping fashion until they fill the bowl to the rim. This may be done ahead of time.

AT THE TABLE   Carefully flip the molded melon sandwiches into a fire pot or cook-and-serve casserole. Lift the bowl slowly, leaving the melon slices nicely arranged in a mound in the pot. Gently add the chicken stock to the pot so that it does not disturb the stacked melon slices. Slowly bring the stock to a boil and simmer for 10 minutes. Serve hot. If a fire pot is used, keep it on low heat and it will remain warm throughout the meal.

Yield: 6 servings as a soup

Variations:

To make a simplified version of this soup, add the sliced winter melon without parboiling to the chicken broth and cook until tender. Add the cut-up ham slices just before serving. To make this soup a little fancier and to give it a slightly different flavor, add a few dried Chinese mushrooms that have been soaked in hot water for $1/2$ hour.

SAN SZU T'ANG
Tri-Colored Clear Soup

INGREDIENTS

8 dried mushrooms
²/₃ cup finely shredded winter bamboo shoots
4 cups vegetable stock or soup, page 10
2 eggs
¹/₄ teaspoon salt
3 teaspoons peanut or corn oil
1 teaspoon sesame oil

PREPARATION

Wash the mushrooms and soak in 1 cup warm water for 30 minutes. Drain and reserve the water from the mushrooms. Remove the residue and add the mushroom water to the stock. Cut off and discard the stems of the mushrooms. Cut the caps into shreds. Set aside with the shredded bamboo shoots. Beat the eggs thoroughly with ¹/₄ teaspoon salt and 1 teaspoon peanut or corn oil.

COOKING

To prevent sticking when cooking the egg sheets, heat an 8-inch skillet until very hot. Add the remaining 2 teaspoons peanut or corn oil to coat all around the surface, then pour out the oil. Turn off the heat and let the skillet completely cool down before cooking in it. To cook the egg sheets, heat the treated skillet. Add ¹/₂ of the beaten eggs and swirl the mixture around the pan to make an 8-inch egg sheet or crepe. When the egg sheet is set, turn it over and brown lightly. Transfer it to a plate. Make the second sheet in the same manner. Cut the egg sheets, one at a time, in 2-inch-wide strips. Stack the pieces and cut again into fine shreds. Set aside with the mushrooms and bamboo shoots. Up to this point, the soup can be prepared ahead.

AT THE TABLE   Pour the vegetable stock into the fire pot or a cook-and-serve casserole and bring it to a boil. Add the cut vegetables and egg sheets and boil for 2 minutes. Add the sesame oil just before serving. Serve hot.

Yield: 8 servings as a soup

Variations:

2 or 3 snow pea pods or a few thin slices of carrots cut into shreds may be added to provide additional color and texture.

HUN TUN HUO KUO
Won Ton Fire Pot

INGREDIENTS

4 cups soy sauce broth, page 12
40 boiled won tons, page 110
2 sheets dried laver (purple seaweed), torn into 1-inch squares
1 recipe shredded egg sheets, page 97

AT THE TABLE

Pour the soy sauce broth into a fire pot or a cook-and-serve casserole and bring it to a boil. Add the boiled won tons and cook until the liquid comes to a boil again. Add the laver and shredded egg sheets. Stir and serve immediately.

Yield: 4 servings as a light meal

Side Dishes, Sauces, and Dips

TOU FAN
Rice with Peas

An easy to make and delicious rice dish to accompany a fire pot dinner.

INGREDIENTS

1 cup rice, preferably short-grain*
1³/₄ cups water
1 cup fresh or frozen peas
¹/₄ cup diced Smithfield ham or 1 Chinese sausage, cut up
¹/₂ teaspoon salt
2 tablespoons peanut or corn oil

PREPARATION

In a heavy saucepan with a tight-fitting lid, add the rice and water and bring to a boil. Cook on high heat about 3 to 4 minutes or until the rice has almost absorbed all the water, but is still boiling with water bubbles. Add the peas and ham or sausage, stir, then add the salt and oil and stir to mix well. Cover and lower the heat to a simmer. Cook for 20 minutes. Turn off the heat, but do not remove from the stove nor lift the lid. Let the rice steam for 10 minutes.

Yield: 4 servings

Variations:

Other salty meats, such as corned beef or fried bacon strips, may be used instead of Smithfield ham. To make this rice dish fancy, add 1 cup diced sautéed fresh mushrooms to the above recipe. Vegetarians can substitute sautéed fresh mushrooms for ham, and increase the salt to 1 teaspoon.

*Available in Japanese and Spanish markets

KUO PA
Puffed Rice Patties

Puffed rice patties are a most delicious and inexpensive snack. They can be served with cocktails and also make an interesting contribution to a fire pot soup.

INGREDIENTS

1¹/₂ cups long-grain rice
2   cups cold water
3   cups peanut or corn oil for deep frying

PREPARATION

Wash and drain the rice several times. Put the rice and cold water in a 10 × 15-inch jelly roll pan and spread the rice evenly to make a thin layer. (If a smaller pan is used, adjust the quantities of rice and water accordingly.) There should be about two layers of rice, and the kernels should be close together. Let stand for 30 minutes. Preheat the oven to 375°.

COOKING

Cover the pan with aluminum foil and bake in the oven for 30 minutes. Remove the foil, moisten the back of a spatula, and lightly press the rice down. Reduce the heat to 325°, and continue baking the rice, uncovered, for about 1 hour. The rice should be dry at the sides of the pan, but the center will still be damp.

Let the rice patties dry at room temperature for 24 hours, or until they are thoroughly dry. Break the dried rice patties into approximately 2 × 2-inch pieces. These dried rice patties can be kept in a cannister or covered container for a long time and fried when needed.

Fry the dried rice patties in very hot oil (about 400°) in a wok, skillet, or deep fryer, two pieces at a time for about 5 seconds on both sides. Drain. The rice patties will puff up, double in size, and will be light brown and crispy. For snacks or appetizers, sprinkle on fine salt while the puffed rice patties are still warm. Do not salt when they are to be added to sizzling rice soup or another fire pot soup. The puffed rice patties can be kept crisp in a tightly covered container for weeks.

Variation:

Oval grain or glutinous rice may be cooked in the same way, using $1/2$ cup less water.

MIEN CHIN
Homemade Wheat Gluten
Balls

Wheat gluten, a uniquely processed food, is made by rinsing the starch out of wheat flour dough. Although it is not difficult to make, it is generally considered more sophisticated than most soy bean products and, as such, it is often used as an ingredient for vegetarian banquet dishes. With its porous texture, it readily absorbs flavors and tastes of other foods. Fried wheat gluten can either be stuffed with meat or left plain and cooked in rich stock with or without vegetables.

INGREDIENTS

3   cups unbleached or all-purpose flour
2   teaspoons salt
1   teaspoon baking powder
$1\frac{1}{8}$ cups warm water (approximately)

PREPARATION

Combine the dry ingredients in a mixing bowl. Make a well and slowly add the warm water, stirring and mixing in the center of the bowl until a soft dough forms. Knead the dough with your hands until it becomes smooth and elastic. If an electric mixer is used, use the dough hook and mix the flour and water slowly. Knead with the hook until the dough is elastic and shiny. Soak the kneaded dough in cold water for at least two hours.

To rinse the dough:

Rinse the dough in a pan of cold water. Squeeze the dough as if you were rinsing a piece of sponge, so that the starch can be rinsed away. Use a strainer when pouring off the water. Change the water frequently and rinse the dough until the water becomes clear. At this point the gluten can be soaked in cold water and refrigerated or frozen and defrosted when needed. Gluten is usually not eaten alone or without complementary ingredients. There are three ways of preparing the gluten before cooking it with the other ingredients: deep frying, boiling, and steaming.

Deep-fried gluten:

Using a wok, heavy pan, or deep fryer, heat 2 cups of oil until it is medium hot or about 350°. Break off a 1-inch lump of gluten and stretch it to the size of a silver dollar. Drop it in the hot oil. Repeat procedure, but fry only a few pieces at a time. The fried gluten will float and puff up. Turn the pieces frequently so that they fry evenly to form golden color balls about 2 inches in diameter. The fried gluten can be frozen or refrigerated for weeks.

Boiled and steamed gluten:

Gluten can be boiled or steamed in one piece, or it can be broken into 1-inch lumps. Drop into boiling water or put on a greased plate to steam. Both methods require at least 1 hour of cooking. The gluten pieces should be fluffy and not chewy. The boiled and steamed gluten balls taste best when they are later braised in soy sauce.

Yield: 24 to 26 wheat gluten balls

YIN CHEN MIEN
Silver Needle Noodles

INGREDIENTS

1 cup wheat starch
²/₃ cup boiling water (approximately)
¹/₄ teaspoon salt

PREPARATION

Put the wheat starch in a mixing bowl. Add the boiling water to the starch stirring with chopsticks or a fork. Then knead it with your hands until it forms a soft smooth ball. If it is sticky, add more starch. Do not overknead or it will become rubbery. Place the dough in a bowl and cover with a piece of cloth and let it rest for 10 minutes.

Divide the dough into 6 portions. Roll each portion into ropelike strips and break into peanut-size bits. Roll each bit again into the shape of a miniature knitting needle, ¹/₄ inch thick and 2 inches long. They should look like silver needle or pin noodles. Put the finished noodles on a greased plate and steam for 5 minutes. The noodles can be added to fire pot soups or to stir-fried dishes.

Yield: 1¹/₂ cups silver needle noodles

HUA CHUAN
Steamed Flower Buns

INGREDIENTS

3¹/₂ cups all-purpose flour (approximately)
1   envelope active dry yeast
1¹/₄ cup lukewarm water
2   teaspoons sugar
1   tablespoon sesame or peanut oil

PREPARATION

Place the flour in a large mixing bowl. Sprinkle the yeast into the lukewarm water. Add sugar and mix and let stand for 5 minutes. Gradually stir the yeast mixture into the flour, forming a firm dough. (Add more flour if dough is sticky.) Knead until smooth and leave in the bowl. Cover the bowl and let rise in a warm place for about 2 hours.

Turn out the dough onto a lightly floured surface and knead until smooth and not sticky, about 7 to 8 minutes. Sprinkle flour onto the dough from time to time while kneading. Divide the dough into half. Put one half in a covered bowl. Roll out the other half into a rectangle, approximately 10 × 14 inches, and about ¹/₈ inch thick. With a pastry brush lightly spread a thin coat of oil over the surface of the dough. Roll up the long side of the dough, jelly-roll fashion, into a long sausagelike shape, about 1 inch in diameter. Cut the roll into pieces ³/₄ inches long. By placing one on top of another, stack pairs of the round pieces, uncut surfaces touching. With the blunt edge of a knife, press down firmly on each pair to make the rounds adhere to each other. Holding the ends of the rounds together with your thumb and forefingers, gently pull the ends slightly away from the center of the roll and then draw the ends under until they meet. Pinch the ends firmly together to secure them. During this process the oiled layers should separate into rosebudlike ''flowers.'' Place the flower buns on a lightly floured tray. Cover with a dry cloth and let rise for 20 minutes.

Repeat with the other half of the dough. Knead again and slightly sprinkle with flour during kneading before shaping into flower buns.

Fill the steamer with 2 to 3 inches water and bring to a boil. Transfer the buns to an oiled rack in the steamer. Do not place buns too close to each other—allow room for rising. You may use two steamer tiers and steam at the same time. Cover the steamer and steam the buns for 10 minutes. Meanwhile, spread a large cloth towel on the table. Immediately transfer the steamed buns to the towel. This will absorb the extra droplets of moisture on the buns. Serve hot.

To store, let them cool completely before putting them into a plastic bag or container. They can be kept in the refrigerator for a week and in a freezer for months. To reheat, put in a steamer and steam for 5 to 10 minutes.

Yield: 30 to 35 buns, 2 × 3 inches

HUN TUN
Won Tons

Won tons are a versatile snack food. In China they are always served in a broth. If there are any left, they are reheated by pan frying with a little oil. Won tons may be served for breakfast, lunch, afternoon, and even midnight snacks. Like hamburgers, they can be eaten at any time of the day. When won tons were brought to the United States, the Chinese began serving them in two additional ways: in a soup before the main course and deep-fried as appetizers. Won tons are made of flour dough wrappers that cover a filling. The flour dough is rolled out into a thin sheet and cut into approximately 3 × 3-inch square wrappers. The filling is usually made of ground pork, and sometimes it is combined with vegetables. To make them extra fancy, ground chicken breast, chopped shrimp, or crab meat can be added to the filling. Depending upon the region, the won ton was originally garnished with different ingredients, such as *laver* (purple seaweed), Szechuan *cha ts'ai* (preserved vegetable), dried shrimp, fried garlic slivers, chopped raw scallion, and other ingredients that give a tang to the won ton.

Won tons are also used as a garnish. For example, a bowl of plain noodles in soy sauce broth can be topped with a few won tons. Since the meat is the most expensive ingredient in won tons and only three or four won tons are used in most dishes, they make light economical snacks.

Making won tons may seem like a tedious process, but after you have mastered the technique, you can make enough won tons for a couple of delicious hot instant meals in 2 to 3 hours. They freeze well. When you make won tons you should always plan to make more than enough for one meal.

Store the extra ones in the freezer. Frozen won tons may be cooked by dropping them into boiling water without defrosting them first.

1   pound ready-made won ton wrappers (75 to 120 pieces depending upon the thickness) or Canton eggroll wrappers

Filling:

1   pound ground pork
1   teaspoon salt
2   teaspoons cornstarch
2   tablespoons light soy sauce
4   tablespoons canned chicken broth
2   teaspoons minced scallion (optional)
$^1/_8$ teaspoon white pepper

If egg wrappers are used, stack them neatly and cut into four squares about 2 × 3-inches. Combine the filling ingredients in a large mixing bowl and stir in one direction until the meat holds together. Before starting to wrap the won tons, have a cup of cold water ready and a damp cloth to cover the wrappers. This will prevent them from drying out while you are making the won tons. One pound of ground pork can fill 80 to 100 won tons.

To stuff and wrap the won tons:

Place 1 teaspoon filling just below the center of the wrapper towards a corner. Fold the corner over the filling and roll toward the center, leaving 1 inch of the opposite corner unrolled. Dip a finger into the cold water and moisten one end of the rolled wrapper. Take the two rolled ends in the fingers of both hands and pull them toward each other until the ends meet and overlap. Pinch the ends firmly together to seal. As each won ton is finished, place it on a tray and cover with a dry towel until ready to cook. At this stage the won tons can also be frozen. They will keep in the freezer for several weeks. When ready to serve, cook in boiling water for 2 minutes longer than usual without defrosting.

To cook the won tons:

In a large pot bring 2 quarts of water or more to a rolling boil. Drop the desired number of won tons (not more than 40 per 2 quarts water). Stir and bring to a boil. Add 1 cup cold water and bring to a boil, and add 1 cup cold water a second time. When the won tons float to the surface, they are done. Remove from the boiling water with a strainer and serve. The cooked won tons may be stored for a couple of days in the refrigerator. Rinse in cold water to separate them before adding to soup.

Yield: 80 to 100 won tons

CHIH MA SHAO PING
Sesame Seed Pastries

INGREDIENTS

1 package active dry yeast
1½ cups lukewarm water
2 teaspoons sugar
4 cups all-purpose flour
3 tablespoons peanut butter
1 teaspoon salt
¼ cup white or black sesame seeds

PREPARATION

Dissolve the yeast in lukewarm water. Add sugar, mix, and let stand for 2 minutes. Place the flour in a large mixing bowl. Add the dissolved yeast to the flour to make a soft, but not sticky, dough and knead it until it feels smooth. Cover with a damp cloth and let rise in a warm place for about 30 minutes.

Knead the dough on a lightly floured surface for 5 minutes. Divide the dough into halves and roll each half into a large rectangular sheet about ¼ inch thick, 14 inches long, and 8 inches wide. Spread the peanut butter evenly over the dough and then sprinkle on the salt. Roll lengthwise jelly-roll fashion to make two 1½-inch-diameter cylinders. Cut each cylinder into 10 pieces. You should have a total of 20 pieces. Pinch each piece at both ends to seal. Lay each piece with pinched side down, then roll each one out into a

3-inch-diameter pattie. Brush each pastry with water, then sprinkle with sesame seeds. Lightly roll with the rolling pin so that the seeds are pressed in. The finished uncooked pastries can be kept in the freezer. Bring to room temperature before cooking.

COOKING Place the pastries in 2 or 3 large skillets. Cover and let set for 20 minutes. Now turn the heat on to low for about 10 minutes. Shake the pans several times with the covers on. By now the bottom of each pastry will be lightly browned. Turn over, cover, and brown the sesame seed sides for 10 minutes. Serve hot.

Yield: 20 sesame seed pastries

Note:

The pastries may be wrapped in foil and reheated in a 350° oven for 15 minutes.

Variation:

Combine $1/2$ cup cooked and finely chopped bacon or ham, $1/2$ cup finely chopped scallion, $1/4$ cup lard or vegetable shortening, and mix well. Spread this evenly on the dough instead of using peanut butter.

T'ANG T'SU CHIEH TS'AI HSIN
Sweet and Sour Mustard Greens

Sweet and sour mustard greens are often served as an accompanying side dish with fire pot dinners.

INGREDIENTS

4 cups hearts of Chinese mustard greens, with outer leaves reserved for soup
1 teaspoon salt
5 tablespoons sugar
4 tablespoons distilled white vinegar
1 teaspoon peanut or corn oil

PREPARATION

Wash the mustard green hearts and allow them to dry completely. Cut them into small 1 × 2-inch pieces. Place the cut up vegetable in a large bowl. Spread and mix the salt to cover all the pieces. Let them stand for an hour.

Drain off and discard the liquid from the salting. Heat the sugar, vinegar, and oil and bring it to a boil. Pour the hot dressing over the salted mustard greens and mix well. Spread and cool; then put the greens into a glass jar, covering tightly, and place it in the refrigerator to pickle for 1 week. Only a small amount is eaten at a time, and it will keep for 1 month.

Yield: 1½ cups pickled mustard greens

Variation:

Celery cabbage may be used instead of mustard greens. Using 1 teaspoon crushed red chili peppers, fry in the oil first, then add the sugar and vinegar and bring to a boil. Continue following the recipe. This dish will have a hot chili pepper flavor instead of a mustard flavor.

CHIANG HUANG KUA
Fresh Cucumbers in Soy Sauce

INGREDIENTS

2 large cucumbers
$^1/_2$ teaspoon salt
1 tablespoon sugar
$^1/_4$ cup light soy sauce
Sesame oil

PREPARATION

Wash the cucumbers well. Cut off and discard both ends. Cut each cucumber lengthwise into two pieces. Remove and discard the seeds and pith. Place the cucumber halves with the skin side up on a cutting board. Score into very thin, attached slices. Cut through every third- or half-inch interval making bite-size pieces.

Place the cut cucumber in a glass jar with a rustproof cover or in a bowl. Sprinkle with the salt, cover, and shake the jar or mix well in the bowl to coat the salt evenly. Set aside 1 hour Drain off the salting liquid. Add the sugar and soy sauce and mix well. The freshly pickled cucumbers may be served right away topped with some of the sesame oil as a side dish, or they may be kept in the refrigerator to be used whenever needed. They will keep for a long time.

Yield: 1 cup pickled cucumbers

Variations:

Chinese white turnip may be used instead of cucumbers. Do not peel, just clean, and cut into small strips or slices. Peeled broccoli stems, carrots, green kohlrabi, or young gingerroot may be pickled in the same way without salting

HSIEN YA TAN
Salted Duck Eggs

INGREDIENTS

1 dozen duck eggs, at room temperature
1 cup coarse salt
5 cups cold water

PREPARATION

In a wide-mouth jar, dissolve the salt in the water and put the duck eggs in the solution. Place a small saucer or a hard plastic cover in the jar, and top it with a stone to weigh down the floating eggs. The eggs must be completely submerged in the brine so that all of them will be evenly salted. Seal the jar with wax paper only; tie with a string or rubber band. This gives the eggs some ventilation so that mold will not form and yet prevents fast evaporation of the water. Keep the covered jar in a cool place. Allow 6 to 8 weeks for salt to penetrate into the eggs. The duration of the salting period depends on the following: the weather—faster in warmer weather; the quality of the egg shells; and the degree of saltiness.

When the eggs are ready for eating, take them out as needed and let the remaining eggs soak in the brine. If they are not salty enough, just leave them in the brine a few more days. If the eggs should become too salty, take the eggs out of the brine and soak in fresh water for a few hours or overnight before cooking.

COOKING Cook the duck eggs in their shells in boiling water for 15 minutes. The traditional way of serving boiled salted eggs is to cut the cooked eggs through the shell into four sections and serve on a plate in wedges. Since they are quite salty, they are eaten in small bits by digging pieces out of the shell with chopsticks. This side dish makes an excellent finishing touch to a fire pot dinner.

Variations:

Chicken, pheasant, double-yolk eggs, or any kind of eggs can be salted. In China, duck eggs are most often salted. The duck and pheasant eggs have richer yolks if salted properly. A rich orange color oil will ooze out of the yolks of cooked eggs. Chicken eggs are less rich, but their whites are more tender. Pheasant eggs only require 5 weeks of salting, but they are not easily available. Duck eggs are not readily found in the markets either. Chicken eggs are just as good for salting, and if double-yolk eggs can be bought, these are even better. The best part of a salted egg is its yolk. Refrigerated salted eggs will keep for months.

TS'UNG YU
Ginger-Scallion Dip

INGREDIENTS

4   scallions, using the white part only
1/2 tablespoon finely minced or grated fresh gingerroot
1/2 teaspoon sugar
1/4 cup peanut or corn oil
1/2 teaspoon cayenne pepper
2   tablespoons light soy sauce or 1 teaspoon salt

PREPARATION

Clean the white parts of the scallions and finely shred them. You should have about 1/2 cup. Put the gingerroot, scallion, and sugar in a heatproof dish.

In a small frying pan, heat the oil and salt, if used, over medium heat until the oil becomes very hot but is not smoking. Add the cayenne pepper. Pour the hot pepper and oil mixture over the gingerroot, scallion, and sugar. Add the light soy sauce or salt to the oil. Mix well. Cool and serve as a dip.

Yield: 1/3 cup

CHIANG MA YU
Sesame-Flavored Soy Sauce Dip

INGREDIENTS

1   tablespoon sesame oil
$1/4$ cup light soy sauce
$1/2$ teaspoon sugar
2   tablespoons chicken broth (optional)

PREPARATION

Combine the sesame oil, soy sauce, and sugar and serve in individual dip dishes or in a saucer. The sauce is concentrated and should be used sparingly. You may add 2 tablespoons chicken broth to dilute the sauce, if you wish.

Yield: $1/3$ cup

Variation:

1 teaspoon fresh garlic paste can be added to the above sauce. Use a mortar and pestle to mash peeled garlic into a paste.

T'ANG TS'U MA YU
Vinegar and Soy Sauce Dip

INGREDIENTS

¹/₄ cup light soy sauce
¹/₄ cup cider vinegar
2 tablespoons sesame oil
2 teaspoons sugar
¹/₄ teaspoon monosodium glutamate

PREPARATION:

Blend ingredients and serve in a sauceboat.

Yield: ²/₃ cup

• 121 •

HSIANG TS'AI YU
Coriander Sauce

INGREDIENTS

3 tablespoons peanut or corn oil
2 teaspoons finely minced gingerroot
$^1/_2$ cup freshly chopped coriander
2 tablespoons light soy sauce
1 teaspoon sugar
$^1/_8$ teaspoon monosodium glutamate

COOKING

Heat a wok until hot and add the oil. Add the gingerroot, stir-fry for 1 minute, then add the coriander, soy sauce, sugar, and monosodium glutamate. Use the sauce as a dip.

Yield: $^1/_2$ cup

T'ANG TS'U CHIANG
Sweet and Sour Sauce

INGREDIENTS

Sauce:

$1/4$ cup distilled white vinegar
$1/4$ cup dry sherry
2 tablespoons soy sauce
2 tablespoons catsup
2 tablespoons water
5 tablespoons sugar
1 tablespoon cornstarch

2 tablespoons peanut or corn oil

PREPARATION

Combine the sauce ingredients in a bowl and set aside.
Heat the oil in a saucepan. Mix the sauce ingredients thoroughly, making sure that the sugar and cornstarch are completely dissolved, and add to the saucepan, stirring constantly. Serve in a sauceboat.

Yield: $1 1/4$ cups

HUA SHENG CHIANG
Peanut Butter and Pepper Sauce

INGREDIENTS

2 tablespoons peanut butter or sesame paste
3 tablespoons warm water
2 tablespoons soy sauce
1 tablespoon cider vinegar
2 tablespoons sesame or corn oil
2 teaspoons hot pepper oil, page 127, or 1 teaspoon cayenne pepper
2 teaspoons sugar
$1/2$ teaspoon salt
$1/4$ teaspoon monosodium glutamate
2 cloves garlic, finely chopped
2 tablespoons finely chopped scallion

PREPARATION

Combine the peanut butter or sesame paste with the warm water to make a smooth, thin sauce. Combine with remaining ingredients except the garlic and scallion into a very smooth dressing. Add the finely chopped garlic and scallion before serving. Serve in a sauceboat.

Yield: $1^1/8$ cups

SZECHUAN TOU PAN CHIANG
Szechuan Hot Pepper Bean Sauce

INGREDIENTS

2 tablespoons crushed red chili peppers
$1/4$ cup hot water
1 pound fresh sweet peppers, preferably the red, finely chopped
1 clove garlic, finely minced
$1/2$ cup corn oil
2 tablespoons brown bean sauce (whole or ground)

PREPARATION

Soak the dried chili peppers with hot water until they are very soft. Drain, reserving the soaking water.

Wash the sweet peppers. Dry thoroughly. Cut and discard the seeds and pith. Chop the peppers and set aside with the minced garlic.

COOKING

Heat the oil in a heavy saucepan until the oil is hot. Add the chili peppers and the garlic, and stir and cook in the oil for 2 minutes. Add the brown bean sauce, sweet peppers, and the soaking water. Bring to a boil and cook together, uncovered, over low heat for about 30 minutes or until the liquid has evaporated, stirring often during this time.

Let cool completely. Keep sauce submerged under the red-hot oil and in a jar with a tight cover at room temperature for weeks, or in the refrigerator indefinitely.

Yield: 1 cup hot chili sauce, to be used as a dip

Note:
The degree of hotness will vary according to the amounts of dried hot peppers added to the sauce; therefore, the proportions of hot and sweet peppers are adjustable according to one's personal taste.

HUA CHIAO YEN
Roasted Salt and Szechuan Peppercorns

INGREDIENTS

¼ cup coarse salt
2 tablespoons Szechuan peppercorns
1 teaspoon whole black peppercorns

COOKING

Roast the salt with the Szechuan peppercorns and whole black peppercorns over medium heat in a dry frying pan. Stir the spices or shake the pan a few times while roasting until the peppercorns are fragrant, about 5 minutes. Cool, then crush with a rolling pin or in a blender.

Strain through a fine sieve. Use the salt and peppercorn mixture sparingly as a dip for fire pot dishes.

Yield: Approximately ¼ cup

LA YU
Hot Pepper Oil

INGREDIENTS

$^{1}/_{2}$ teaspoon ground roasted Szechuan peppercorns*
$^{1}/_{2}$ cup corn oil
2 tablespoons cayenne pepper
1 teaspoon paprika

PREPARATION

Heat a wok and add the corn oil. Heat the oil until it just starts to smoke. Turn off the heat, wait for 30 seconds (for a heavy pan wait a little longer), then add the cayenne pepper, roasted Szechuan peppercorns, and paprika. Stir well and let sit until the solids settle.

Strain the oil through a paper towel-lined strainer. Discard the solids. Store the oil in a jar without refrigerating. Use 1 to 2 teaspoons for a dip according to taste.

Yield: Approximately $^{1}/_{2}$ cup

*To make ground roasted Szechuan peppercorns: roast 1 teaspoon Szechuan peppercorns over medium heat in a dry frying pan for about 5 minutes or until they are fragrant. Cool, then finely grind the peppercorns with a mortar and pestle or in a blender or crush with a rolling pin.

Index